COPYCAT RECIPES

A Step-by-Step Guide to Making the
Most Popular and Favorite Restaurant
Dishes for Beginners. Discover how to
Cook Beautiful Meals for Your Family
Today !

Melissa Pot

© Copyright 2020 by Melissa Pot
- All rights Reserved -

TABLE OF CONTENTS

Introduction

American families adore going out to eat at their favorite restaurants; however, surveys have shown that people are spending less money than ever at restaurants due to budget restrictions and a declining economy. If you are one of those people, why not surprise your family and friends with their favorite restaurant dish by making it at home in your own kitchen?

In reading this, you will realize that you can actually cook at home the recipes that you love the most for a fraction of the cost of dining out. You will find step-by-step instructions for all those amazing dishes that draw people into restaurants, and you will be sure that the food was cooked under hygienic conditions since you will be making it yourself.

You don't have to be a master chef to prepare these meals. All these recipes use basic ingredients that can be found in any grocery store.

Here, you will find tips on how to create the restaurant feeling at home. You'll get a list of basic cookware and appliances you need to have in your kitchen as well as how to stock your pantry to prepare some amazing dishes. There will be a primer on how to choose the best and freshest ingredients. You will also learn the basic cooking terms and techniques used in here.

The Cost of Eating Out

When you pay for a meal at a restaurant, usually you're paying three times more than the actual cost of the ingredients it took to make the food. That's around $14 in a restaurant which would have only cost $4.25 if you had made it yourself. There are four ways restaurant owners' price their menu items. "Cost of raw ingredients" divided by "desired food cost percentage (which is about 25-30%)" equals "the price." This is how the $14 restaurant meal cost was calculated earlier.

The second method is to base the price on competing restaurants. Restaurant owners will either adopt the same price of their competitors, lower the price of their meals for those trying to find a better deal, or raise their prices to appear of higher quality compared to their competition.

The third method of menu pricing is to base prices on supply and demand. For example, the food is usually priced higher at places like sports stadiums and airports simply because they know you will be hungry and thirsty and there aren't a lot of other options. Restaurants that have unique themes to their interior or food can also mark their prices higher since the customers aren't just paying for the food, they're also paying for the overall dining experience.

Finally, the fourth and last pricing method is by evaluating your menu items' profitability. If restaurant owners know that one particular meal is selling well, they will raise the other prices by just a small, infinitesimal amount so that it will increase profitability to balance with the best-sellers. Regardless of the pricing method, when you're eating at a restaurant, you're not just paying for the food but for the restaurants overhead as well.

Copycat restaurant recipes are now widely known because of the ever-high cost of eating out. These copycat restaurant recipes are the hidden recipes from all your favorite restaurants in America so you can prepare them in the comfort of your home.

The benefit of using copycat restaurant recipes is that not only can you save money; you can also customize the recipes. For example, if you want to reduce the salt or butter in one of the plates, you can. Now you've saved money, and at the same time provided a nutritious meal for your family.

You have little control over the ingredients in the meal when you eat out. You can't, of course, adjust the dish that you order because sauces, etc. are made in advance.

All of us know that it is expensive to take our family out for dinner, and without a doubt, this would easily cost you around a hundred dollars on an average. With copycat restaurant recipes the same one hundred dollars can easily produce 4 or more meals.

Now, imagine that you also have all the needed ingredients at home for a second to cook the same food with copycat restaurant recipes. So, when you're making a copycat restaurant recipe you can "wow" your family and guests.

You're going to have them thinking you've picked up dinner from a favorite restaurant just by using these recipes and saving costs compared to dining out.

Trying to guess what the ingredients are to your favorite restaurant meal is eliminated when you use copycat recipes. You simply follow the recipe, and slowly recreate your favorite meal.

Having regular meals inspired by your favorite restaurants as a family allows for a healthier, more tight-knit family. Research have shown that in school, families who dine together at home are more united, happier and the kids perform better.

To sum up, the huge savings you'll gain from cooking at home could be used for more productive things like a family holiday or college tuition for your kids.

Going out for a meal at your favorite restaurant is always fun to most. But what if you had access to the top-secret restaurant recipes that so heavily guard those popular restaurants? Would you go home cooking these yourself whenever you wish?

It is not really that difficult to learn how to cooktop secret restaurant recipes. Some think you need a degree in culinary arts or cooking education so you can cook those secret recipes. I hate telling you this, but anyone can collect the ingredients themselves and cook a fancy meal that tastes like the real thing.

But do top secret restaurant recipes really taste the way the chef served them? Perhaps. You can easily cook your favorite recipes with a little practice and patience.

The advantage of making your own top-secret recipes is that you can add to your recipes your own flavors and spices. You'd just want to cook the basic formula and start adding what you think would make the flavor of the recipe better after a while. You may start to figure out that some recipes might need a little more herbs or peppers to make the dish better than the original!

Cooking top secret recipes from restaurants will also make your friends and family wonder where you've learned to cook so well. Imagine cooking a whole meal that looks like it was the restaurant's take-out food. I bet some friends of yours won't even believe you've cooked it!

Famous Breakfast Recipes

Spinach and Cheese Egg Soufflé from Panera

Preparation Time: 15

Cooking Time: 25

Servings: 4

Ingredients:

1 tube butter flake crescent rolls

6 eggs, divided

2 tablespoons milk

2 tablespoons heavy cream

1/4 cup cheddar cheese, grated

1/4 cup jack cheese, grated

1 tablespoon Parmesan cheese

3 tablespoons fresh spinach, mince

4 slices of bacon, cooked and crumbled

Cooking spray

1/4 teaspoon salt

1/4 cup Asiago cheese, grated, divided

Directions:

Preheat oven to 375°F.

Add 5 eggs, milk, heavy cream, cheddar cheese, jack cheese, parmesan cheese, spinach, bacon, and salt to a nonreactive bowl. Mix well until combined then heat in microwave for about 30 seconds. Stir, then microwave for another 20 seconds. Repeat about 5 times or until egg mixture is a bit thicker but still runny and uncooked.

Roll out crescent roll dough. Make 4 rectangles by pressing together the triangles. Then, using a roll pin, stretch them out until they are 6in x 6in square.

Coat ramekin with cooking spray and place flattened roll inside, making sure the edges are outside the ramekin. Add ⅓ cup egg mixture and then about ⅛ cup Asiago cheese. Wrap edges of the roll-on top. Repeat for remaining rolls.

Whisk remaining egg with salt lightly in a bowl then, with a pastry brush, brush on top of each crescent roll dough.

Place ramekins in the oven and bake for 20 minutes or until brown.

Serve.

Nutrition: Calories: 303 Fat: 25 g Saturated Fat: 11 g Carbs: 4 g Sugar: 1 g Fibers: 0 g Protein: 20 g Sodium: 749 mg

Sonic's SuperSONIC™ Copycat Burrito

Preparation Time: 10 minutes

Cooking Time: 25 minutes

Servings: 8

Ingredients: 50 tater tots, frozen

1-pound breakfast sausage patties - 8 large eggs, beaten

2 tablespoons half and half - Salt and pepper, to taste

1 tablespoon butter - 8 6-inch flour tortillas

1½ cups cheddar cheese, grated - 1 medium onion, diced

½ cup pickled jalapeño peppers, sliced - 3 roma tomatoes, sliced

Salsa

Directions: Cook tater tots per instructions on the package but cook them so they are a bit crispy. Set aside. In a pan, cook sausage patties. Break apart into large clumps until brown.

Add eggs, half and half, salt, and pepper in a bowl. Whisk until well mixed.

Heat butter in a pan over medium heat. Pour egg mixture and stir every now and then until scrambled Remove from heat.

Microwave tortillas until warm but still soft. Then, in a vertical line in the center, add cheddar cheese, eggs, cooked sausage, tater tots, onions, jalapeños, and tomato. Fold the ingredients using the outer flaps of the tortilla. Repeat with remaining ingredients and tortillas.

Serve warm with salsa.

Nutrition: Calories: 636 Fat: 40 g Saturated Fat: 16 g Carbs: 39 g Sugar: 4 g Fibers: 3 g Protein: 28 g Sodium: 1381 mg

Cracker Barrel's Biscuits

Preparation Time: 15 minutes

Cooking Time: 8 minutes

Servings: 8

Ingredients:

2 cups self-rising flour

⅓ cup shortening

⅔ cup buttermilk

Melted butter, to brush

Directions:

Preheat oven to 450 °F.

In a bowl, mix flour and shortening until mixture is loose and crumbly.

Pour in buttermilk. Mix well.

Sprinkle flour onto a smooth surface and flatten dough on top. Cut dough into desired shapes using biscuit cutters.

Arrange onto a baking sheet. Place in oven and cook for 8 minutes. Apply melted butter on top using a brush.

Serve.

Nutrition: Calories: 194 Fat: 9 g Carbs: 24 g Protein: 4 g Sodium: 418 mg

The Spinach and Artichoke Dip from Applebee's

Preparation Time: 5 minutes

Cooking Time: 30 minutes

Servings: 10

Ingredients:

1 10-ounce bag spinach, diced

2 14-ounce cans artichoke hearts, diced

1 cup Parmesan-Romano cheese mix, grated

2 cups mozzarella cheese, grated

16 ounces garlic alfredo sauce

8 ounces cream cheese, softened

Directions:

Combine all ingredients in a bowl. Mix well.

Transfer into a slow cooker. Set on high and cook for 30 minutes.

Serve while hot.

Nutrition: Calories: 228 Fat: 15 g Carbs: 12 g Protein: 13 g Sodium: 418 mg

Copycat Mozzarella Sticks from TGI Fridays

Preparation Time: 10 minutes

Cooking Time: 5 minutes

Servings: 16

Ingredients:

⅔ cup all-purpose flour

2 large eggs

¼ cup milk

1 cup Japanese breadcrumbs

½ cup Parmesan cheese, shredded

1 tablespoon dried parsley

½ teaspoon garlic salt

½ teaspoon seasoning salt

8 pieces mozzarella string cheese

1-quart vegetable oil

Marinara sauce

Directions:

Add flour to a bowl. Then, in a separate bowl, mix eggs and milk. Add breadcrumbs, Parmesan, parsley, garlic salt, and seasoning salt in a third bowl and mix well.

Line baking sheet with wax paper. Set aside.

Cut mozzarella pieces in half vertically so that you will end up with 16 mozzarella sticks. Then, for each piece, dredge first in flour, followed by egg wash, and third in breadcrumb mixture. Dredge again in egg wash and breadcrumbs for a thicker coat. Place pieces on prepared baking sheet and place in freezer for at least 1 hour or overnight.

To prepare mozzarella sticks preheat deep fryer to 350°F.

About 4 sticks at a time, deep fry for about 30 seconds or until golden brown. Using a slotted spoon, transfer to a rack or plate lined with paper towels to drain.

Serve warm with marinara sauce.

Nutrition: Calories: 118 Fat: 7 g Saturated Fat: 4 g Carbs: 8 g Sugar: 1g Fiber: 0g Protein: 7 g Sodium: 340 mg

The French Toasts from Denny's

Preparation Time: 10 minutes

Cooking Time: 12 minutes

Servings: 6

Ingredients:

Batter:

4 eggs

⅔ cup whole milk

⅓ cup flour

⅓ cup sugar

½ teaspoon vanilla extract

¼ teaspoon salt

⅛ teaspoon cinnamon

Other ingredients

6 slices bread loaf, sliced thick

3 tablespoons butter

Powdered sugar for dusting

Syrup as desired

Directions:

Mix in the ingredients for batter in a bowl.

Soak bread slices in batter one at a time for at least 30 seconds on both sides. Allow excess batter to drip off. Melt 1 tablespoon of butter in a pan, cook battered bread over medium heat for 2 minutes or until each side is golden brown. Move slice to a plate.

Repeat with the remaining slices of bread, adding more butter to the pan if needed.

Dust with powdered sugar, if desired, and with syrup poured on top.

Nutrition: Calories: 264 Fat: 11 g Carbs: 33 g Protein: 8 g Sodium: 360 mg

IHOP's Healthy "Harvest Grain 'N Nut" Pancakes

Preparation Time: 5 minutes

Cooking Time: 5 minutes

Servings: 4

Ingredients: 1 teaspoon olive oil - ¾ cup oats, powdered

¾ cup whole wheat flour - 2 teaspoons baking soda

1 teaspoon baking powder - ½ teaspoon salt

1½ cup buttermilk - ¼ cup vegetable oil - 1 egg - ¼ cup sugar

3 tablespoons almonds, finely sliced

3 tablespoons walnuts, sliced

Syrup for serving

Directions: Heat oil in a pan over medium heat.

As pan preheats, pulverize oats in a blender until powdered. Then, add to a large bowl with flour, baking soda, baking powder and salt. Mix well.

Add buttermilk, oil, egg, and sugar in a separate bowl. Mix with an electric mixer until creamy.

Mix in wet ingredients with dry ingredients, then add nuts. Mix everything together with electric mixer.

Scoop ⅓ cup of batter and cook in the hot pan for at least 2 minutes or until both sides turn golden brown. Transfer onto a plate, then repeat for the remaining batter. Serve with syrup.

Nutrition: Calories: 433 Fat: 24 g Carbs: 46 g Protein: 12 g Sodium: 1128 mg

McDonald's Sausage Egg McMuffin

Preparation Time: 10 minutes

Cooking Time: 15 minutes

Servings: 4

Ingredients:

4 English muffins, cut in half horizontally

4 slices American processed cheese

½ tablespoon oil

1-pound ground pork, minced

½ teaspoon dried sage, ground

½ teaspoon dried thyme

1 teaspoon onion powder

¾ teaspoon black pepper

¾ teaspoon salt

½ teaspoon white sugar

4 large ⅓-inch onion ring slices

4 large eggs

2 tablespoons water

Directions:

Preheat oven to 300°F.

Cover one half of muffin with cheese, leaving one half uncovered. Transfer both halves to a baking tray. Place in oven.

For the sausage patties, use your hands to mix pork, sage, thyme, onion powder, pepper, salt, and sugar in a bowl. Form into 4 patties. Make sure they are slightly larger than the muffins.

Heat oil in a pan. Cook patties on both sides for at least 2 minutes each or until all sides turn brown. Remove tray of muffins from oven. Place cooked sausage patties on top of the cheese on muffins. Return tray to the oven.

In the same pan, position onion rings flat into a single layer. Crack one egg inside each of the onion rings to make them round. Add water carefully into the sides of the pan and cover. Cook for 2 minutes.

Remove tray of muffins from the oven. Add eggs on top of patties, then top with the other muffin half.

Serve warm.

Nutrition: Calories: 453 Fat: 15 g Carbs: 67 g Protein: 15 g Sodium: 1008 mg

Starbucks' Spinach and Feta Breakfast Wraps

Preparation Time: 5 minutes

Cooking Time: 20 minutes

Servings: 6

Ingredients: 10 ounces spinach leaves

1 14½-ounce can dice tomatoes, drained

3 tablespoons cream cheese - 10 egg whites - ½ teaspoon oregano

½ teaspoon garlic salt - ⅛ teaspoon pepper

6 whole wheat tortillas - 4 tablespoons feta cheese, crumbled

Cooking Spray

Directions:

Apply light coating of cooking spray to a pan. Cook spinach leaves on medium-high heat for 5 minutes or until leaves wilt, then stir in tomatoes and cream cheese. Cook for an additional 5 minutes or until cheese is melted completely. Remove from pan and place into glass bowl and cover. Set aside.

In the same pan, add egg whites, oregano, salt, and pepper. Stir well and cook at least 5 minutes or until eggs are scrambled. Remove from heat.

Microwave tortillas for 30 seconds or until warm. Place egg whites, spinach and tomato mixture, and feta in the middle of the tortillas. Fold sides inwards, like a burrito. Serve.

Nutrition: Calories: 157 Fat: 3 g Carbs: 19 g Protein: 14 g Sodium: 305 mg

Jimmy Dean's Homemade Pork Sage Sausage

Preparation Time: 5 minutes

Cooking Time: 20 minutes

Servings: 4

Ingredients:

1-pound ground pork

1 teaspoon salt

½ teaspoon dried parsley

¼ teaspoon rubbed sage

¼ teaspoon black pepper, ground

¼ teaspoon dried thyme

¼ teaspoon coriander

¼ teaspoon seasoned salt

Directions:

Mix all ingredients in a bowl.

Shape into patties. Then, cook in a pan on medium heat until meat is brown on both sides and cooked through.

Serve.

Nutrition: Calories: 313 Fat: 24 g Carbs: 4 g Protein: 19 g Sodium: 646 mg

Baked Oatmeal for a Crowd with Berries and Seeds

Preparation Time: 20 minutes

Cooking Time: 50 minutes

Servings: 8

Ingredients: 4 tablespoons unsalted butter, melted, plus more for pan

6 medjool dates, pitted and chopped (1/2 cup)

4 cups old fashioned rolled oats - 1 teaspoon baking powder

1/2 teaspoon kosher salt - 1/2 teaspoon ground cinnamon

4 cups whole milk - 1/4 cup pure maple syrup, plus more

for serving

2 large eggs - 2 teaspoons pure vanilla extract

1 cup fresh or frozen mixed berries - 1/4 cup toasted pepitas

2 tablespoons hemp seed hearts

Directions:

Step 1: Heat oven to 350°F. Butter a 3-quart baking dish. Sprinkle dates evenly along bottom. In a large bowl, whisk together oats, baking powder, salt, and cinnamon. In another bowl, combine milk, maple syrup, melted butter, eggs, and vanilla extract. Add to bowl with oats and stir to combine. Transfer to prepared dish.

Step2: Sprinkle top with berries and bake until just set, about 35 minutes. Sprinkle pepitas and hemp hearts over oatmeal. Let cool 20 minutes. Serve warm or cold with extra maple syrup, if desired. Baked oatmeal can be stored covered in the refrigerator up to 5 days.

Nutrition: Calories: 312 Fat: 26g Carbs: 4g Protein: 18 g Sodium: 356g

DIY California A.M. Crunchwrap

Preparation Time: 10 minutes

Cooking Time: 20 minutes

Servings: 4

Ingredients: 4 frozen hash brown patties

5 large eggs - 1 tablespoon milk

Salt and pepper, to taste

4 large tortillas - 1 cup cheddar cheese, shredded

4 strips of thick cut bacon, cooked and crumbled

2 ripe California avocados, peeled and pitted

4 tablespoons pico de gallo

Directions:

Cook hash brown patties until crisp, based on package instructions.

Add eggs, milk, salt, and pepper in a bowl. Mix well until combined. Then, pour onto a skillet and cook until scrambled. Set aside.

Heat two different-sized (one smaller than other) heavy bottomed pans over medium heat. Once heated, place tortillas into the bigger pan and, in even amounts, add cheese, a hash brown patty, eggs, bacon, avocado, and pico de gallo in the center of the tortilla in that order.

Using a wheel pattern, fold tortilla around the filling with the edge facing up. Place heated smaller pan (such as a cast iron skillet) on top for about 20 seconds or until browned. Serve immediately.

Nutrition: Calories: 933 Fat: 51 g Saturated Fat: 15 g Carbs: 91 g Sugar: 1 g Fibers: 11 g Protein: 32 g Sodium: 1343 mg

Appetizers I

Pei Wei's Crab Wonton

Preparation Time: 10 minutes

Cooking Time: 5 minutes

Servings: 6

Ingredients:

1 (7-ounce) can white crab meat

½ pound cream cheese, softened

2-3 green onions, sliced

½ tablespoon garlic powder

Splash of soy sauce

Wonton wrappers

Cooking oil

Directions:

Combine the crab, cream cheese, green onions, garlic powder and soy sauce in a bowl. Stir until the mixture reaches a paste-like consistency.

Spoon a bit of the mixture into each wonton wrapper and fold. Seal around the edges with a moistened finger.

Nutrition: Calories: 244 Fat: 15 g Carbs: 34 g Protein: 87 g Sodium: 344 g

Pei Wei's Vietnamese Chicken Salad Spring Roll

Preparation Time: 10 minutes

Cooking Time: 1 minutes

Servings: 4-6

Ingredients:

Salad

Rice Wrappers

Green leaf lettuce like Boston Bibb lettuce

Napa cabbage, shredded

Green onions, chopped

Mint, chopped

Carrots, cut into 1-inch matchsticks

Peanuts

Chicken, diced and cooked, about 6 chicken tenders drizzled with soy sauce, honey, garlic powder, and red pepper flakes

Lime dressing

2 tablespoons lime juice, about 1 lime

1½ teaspoons water

1 tablespoon sugar

1 teaspoon salt

Dash of pepper

3 tablespoons oil

Add everything but the oil to a small container or bowl and shake or stir until the sugar and salt are dissolved. Next, add the oil and shake well.

Peanut dipping sauce

2 tablespoons soy sauce

1 tablespoon rice wine vinegar

2 tablespoons brown sugar

¼ cup peanut butter

1 teaspoon chipotle Tabasco

1 teaspoon honey

1 teaspoon sweet chili sauce

1 teaspoon lime vinaigrette

Add all the ingredients to a small bowl and mix to combine thoroughly.

Directions:

In a large bowl, mix together all of the salad ingredients except for the rice wrappers and lettuce.

Place the rice wrappers in warm water for about 1 minute to soften.

Transfer the wrappers to a plate and top each with 2 pieces of lettuce.

Top the lettuce with the salad mixture and drizzle with the lime dressing. Fold the wrapper by tucking in the ends and then rolling.

Serve with lime dressing and peanut dipping sauce.

Nutrition: Calories: 178 Fat: 4.4 g Carbs: 7 g Protein: 68 g Sodium: 357 g

Takeout Dry Garlic Ribs

Preparation Time: 15 minutes

Cooking Time: 2 hours and 15 minutes

Servings: 4-6

Ingredients:

6 pounds pork ribs, silver skin removed and cut into individual ribs

1½ cups broth - 1½ cups brown sugar - ¼ cup soy sauce

12 cloves garlic, minced - ¼ cup yellow mustard

1 large onion, finely chopped - ¼ teaspoon salt

½ teaspoon black pepper

Directions: Preheat oven to 200°F.

Season ribs with salt and pepper and place on a baking tray. Cover with aluminum foil and bake for 1 hour.

In a mixing bowl, stir together the broth, brown sugar, soy sauce, garlic, mustard and onion. Continue stirring until the sugar is completely dissolved.

After an hour, remove the foil from the ribs and turn the heat up to 350°F.

Carefully pour the sauce over the ribs. Re-cover with the foil and return to the oven for 1 hour.

Remove the foil and bake for 15 more minutes on each side.

Nutrition: Calories: 233 Fat: 3.6 g Carbs: 6.4 g Protein:65 g Sodium: 434 g

Abuelo Jalapeno Poppers

Preparation Time: 10 minutes

Cooking Time: 1 hour and 10 minutes

Servings: 8

Ingredients:

30 jalapeno peppers; sliced into half lengthwise

1 cup milk

2 packages soften cream cheese, at room temperature (8-ounces each)

1/8 teaspoon paprika

12 ounces Cheddar cheese, shredded

1/8 teaspoon chili powder

1 cup flour

1/8 teaspoon garlic powder

1 cup seasoned breadcrumbs

¼ teaspoon ground black pepper

1 quart of oil for frying

¼ teaspoon salt

Directions:

Scrape out seeds and the pith inside of the jalapeno peppers using a spoon. Combine cheddar cheese together with cream cheese in a medium-sized bowl; give them a good stir until blended well. Fill each pepper half with the prepared cream cheese blend using a spoon.

Add flour into a small-sized shallow bowl. Add paprika, pepper, garlic powder, chili powder and salt. Blend into the flour until it is mixed. Pour milk into a separate medium-sized shallow bowl. Dip stuffed jalapeno into flour. Place the floured pepper on a large-sized baking sheet with a rack. Let dry for 10 minutes.

Pour the dried breadcrumbs into a separate bowl. Dip the floured jalapeno pepper into the milk & then into the bowl with the breadcrumbs. Place the pepper on the rack again. Preheat the oil to 350 F in advance. Dip pepper into the milk & then into the breadcrumbs. Repeat these steps until you have utilized the entire dipping peppers.

Work in batches and fry peppers for a minute or two, until turn golden brown. Remove from oil & place them on a baking rack to drain.

Nutrition: Calories: 257 Fat: 14. 3 g Carbs: 18.9 g Protein: 21.5 Sodium: 531 mg

Applebee's Baja Potato Boats

Preparation Time:10 minutes

Cooking Time: 30 minutes

Servings: 4

Ingredients:

For Pico de Gallo: 1 ½ teaspoon fresh cilantro, minced

1 tablespoon canned jalapeño slices (nacho slices), diced

3 tablespoons Spanish onion, chopped

1 chopped tomato (approximately ½ cup)

A dash each of freshly-ground black pepper & salt

For the Potato Boats:

2 slices Canadian bacon diced (roughly 2 tablespoons)

Canola oil nonstick cooking spray, as required

⅓ cup Cheddar cheese, shredded - 3 russet potatoes, medium

⅓ cup Mozzarella cheese - salt as needed

On the Side: - Salsa & sour cream

Directions: Combine the entire Pico De Gallo ingredients together in a large bowl; mix well. When done, place in a refrigerator until ready to use.

Preheat your oven to 400 F in advance. Place potatoes in oven & bake until tender, for an hour. Set aside at room temperature until easy to handle. When done, cut them lengthwise 2 times. This should make 3 ½ to ¾" slices, throwing the middle slices away.

Increase your oven's temperature to 450 F. Take a spoon & scoop out the inside of the potato skins. Ensure that you must leave at least ¼ of an inch of the potato inside each skin. Spray the potato skin completely on all sides with the spray of nonstick canola oil. Put the skins, cut-side facing up on a large-sized cookie sheet. Sprinkle them with salt & bake in the preheated oven until the edges start to turn brown, for 12 to 15 minutes.

Combine both the cheeses together in a large bowl. Sprinkle approximately 1 ½ tablespoons of the mixture on each potato skin. Then sprinkle a teaspoon of the Canadian bacon over the cheese. Top this with a large tablespoon of the pico de gallo and then sprinkle each skin with some more of cheese.

Place the skins into the oven again & bake until the cheese melts, for 2 to 4 more minutes. Remove & let them sit for a minute. Slice each one lengthwise using a sharp knife. Serve hot with some salsa and sour cream on the side.

Nutrition: Calories: 254 Fat: 24 g Carbs: 43 g Protein: 55 g Sodium: 779 mg

Applebee's Chicken Wings

Preparation Time: 15 minutes

Cooking Time: 35 minutes

Servings: 6

Ingredients:

35 chicken wings

1 ½ tablespoon flour

3 tablespoons vinegar

1 ¼ teaspoon cayenne pepper

1 tablespoon Worcestershire sauce

12 ounces Louisiana hot sauce

¼ teaspoon garlic powder

Directions:

Cook the chicken wings either by deep-frying or baking.

Mix the entire sauce ingredients (except the flour) together over low-medium heat in a large saucepan. Cook until warm and then add in the flour; stir well until you get your desired level of thickness.

When thick; cover the bottom of 9x13" baking dish with the sauce. Combine the leftover sauce with the cooked wings & place them in the baking dish. Bake until warm, for 15 to 20 minutes, at 300 F.

Serve with blue-cheese dressing and celery sticks. Enjoy.

Nutrition: Calories: 189 Fat: 11 g Carbs: 35 g Protein: 46 g Sodium: 2316 g

Appetizers II

Panda Express's Chicken Potstickers

Preparation Time: 40 minutes

Cooking Time: 30 minutes

Servings: 50

Ingredients:

½ cup + 2 tablespoons soy sauce, divided

1 tablespoon rice vinegar

3 tablespoons chives, divided

1 tablespoon sesame seeds

1 teaspoon sriracha hot sauce

1-pound ground pork

3 cloves garlic, minced

1 egg, beaten

1½ tablespoons sesame oil

1 tablespoon fresh ginger, minced

50 dumpling wrappers

1 cup vegetable oil, for frying

1-quart water

Directions:

In a mixing bowl, whisk together the ½ cup of soy sauce, vinegar, 1 tablespoon of the chives, sesame seeds and sriracha to make the dipping sauce.

In a separate bowl, mix together the pork, garlic, egg, the rest of the chives, the 2 tablespoons of soy sauce, sesame oil and the ginger.

Add about 1 tablespoon of the filling to each dumpling wrapper.

Pinch the sides of the wrappers together to seal. You may need to wet the edges a bit, so they'll stick.

Heat the cup of oil in a large skillet. When hot, working in batches, add the dumplings and cook until golden brown on all sides. Take care of not overloading your pan.

Add the water and cook until tender, then serve with the dipping sauce.

Nutrition: Calories: 182 Fat: 2.3 g Carbs: 19 g Protein: 11.2 g Sodium: 331 g

Panda Express's Cream Cheese Rangoon

Preparation Time: 5 minutes

Cooking Time: 5 minutes

Servings: 24 minutes

Ingredients:

¼ cup green onions, chopped

½ pound cream cheese, softened

½ teaspoon garlic powder

½ teaspoon salt

24 wonton wrappers

Oil for frying

Directions:

Add the green onions, cream cheese, garlic powder and salt to a medium sized bowl and mix together.

Lay the wonton wrappers out and moisten the edges of the first one. Add about ½ tablespoon of filling to the center of the wrapper and seal by pinching the edges together, starting with the corners and working your way inward. Make sure it is sealed tightly. Repeat with the remaining wrappers.

Add about 3 inches of oil to a large pot. Heat it to about 350°F, then add the wontons a few at a time and cook until brown.

Remove from oil and place on a paper-towel-lined plate to drain.

Nutrition: Calories: 193 Fat: 5 g Carbs: 100 g Protein: 11 g Sodium: 123 g

Panda Express's Chicken Egg Roll

Preparation Time: 10 minutes

Cooking Time: 5 minutes

Servings: 6-8

Ingredients: 2 tablespoons soy sauce, divided

2 cloves garlic, minced, divided - 2 green onions, chopped, divided

3 tablespoons vegetable oil, divided

½ pound boneless skinless chicken breasts, cooked whole & cut in pieces

½ head green cabbage, thinly shredded

1 large carrot, peeled and shredded - 1 cup bean sprouts

12-16 egg roll wrappers

1 tablespoon cornstarch mixed with 3 tablespoons water

Peanut Oil for frying

Directions:

In a resealable plastic bag, combine 1 tablespoon of the soy sauce with 1 clove of minced garlic, 1 green onion, and 1 tablespoon of the oil. Mix well. Add the cut-up chicken pieces, seal the bag, and squish it around to make sure the chicken is covered. Refrigerate for at least 30 minutes.

After the chicken has marinated, pour 1 tablespoon of the oil into a large skillet and heat over medium-high heat. When the oil is hot, add the chicken and cook, stirring occasionally, until the chicken is cooked through. Remove the chicken from the skillet and set aside. Pour the remaining tablespoon of oil into the skillet and add the cabbage, carrots and remaining soy sauce. Cook and stir until the carrots and cabbage start to soften, then add the bean sprouts and the remaining garlic and green onions. Cook another minute or so.

Drain the chicken and vegetables thoroughly using either a cheesecloth or a mesh strainer. Getting all the excess liquid out will keep the egg rolls from getting soggy. In a large saucepan or Dutch oven, heat 3 inches of oil to 375°F. Place about 2 tablespoons of the chicken and vegetables into the center of each egg roll wrapper. Fold the ends up and roll up to cover the filling. Seal by dipping your finger in the water and cornstarch mixture and covering the edges.

Cook the egg rolls in batches, a few at a time, for about five minutes or until golden brown and crispy. Remove from oil to a paper-towel-lined plate to drain.

Nutrition: Calories: 349 Fat: 4 g Carbs: 176 g Protein: 13 g Sodium: 340 g

Panda Express's Veggie Spring Roll

Preparation Time: 15 minutes

Cooking Time: 5 minutes

Servings: 6-8

Ingredients:

4 teaspoons vegetable oil, divided

3 eggs, beaten

1 medium head cabbage, finely shredded

½ carrot, julienned

1 (8-ounce) can shredded bamboo shoots

1 cup dried, shredded wood ear mushroom, rehydrated

1-pound Chinese barbecue or roasted pork, cut into matchsticks

½ cup chopped Chinese yellow chives

1 green onion, thinly sliced

2½ teaspoons soy sauce

1 teaspoon salt

1 teaspoon sugar

1 (14-ounce) package egg roll wrappers

1 egg white, beaten

1-quart oil for frying, or as needed

Directions:

In a large skillet, heat 1 tablespoon of oil over medium-high heat.

When the skillet is hot, add the beaten eggs and cook until firm, then flip and cook a bit longer like an omelet. When set, remove from the pan. Cut into strips and set aside.

Add the remaining oil to the skillet and heat. When hot, add the cabbage and carrot and cook for a couple of minutes until they start to soften. Then add the bamboo shoots, mushrooms, pork, green onions, chives, soy sauce, salt and sugar. Cook until the veggies are soft, then stir in the egg. Transfer the mixture to a bowl and refrigerate for about 1 hour.

When cooled, add about 2-3 tablespoons of filling to each egg roll wrapper. Brush some of the beaten egg around the edges of the wrapper and roll up, tucking in the ends first.

When all of the wrappers are filled, heat about 6 inches of oil to 350°F in a deep saucepan, Dutch oven or fryer.

Add the egg rolls to the hot oil a couple at a time. When golden brown and crispy, remove from oil to a paper-towel-lined plate to drain.

Serve with chili sauce or sweet and sour sauce.

Nutrition: Calories: 132 Fat: 3.3 g Carbs: 5.5 g Protein:32 g Sodium: 213 g

PF Chang's Hot and Sour Soup

Preparation Time: 10 minutes

Cooking Time: 10 minutes

Servings: 4-6

Ingredients:

6 ounces chicken breasts, cut into thin strips

1-quart chicken stock

1 cup soy sauce

1 teaspoon white pepper

1 (6 ounce) can bamboo shoots, cut into strips

6 ounces wood ear mushrooms, cut into strips or canned straw mushrooms, if wood ear can't be found

½ cup cornstarch

½ cup water

2 eggs, beaten

½ cup white vinegar

6 ounces silken tofu, cut into strips

Sliced green onions for garnish

Directions:

Cook the chicken strips in a hot skillet until cooked through. Set aside.

Add the chicken stock, soy sauce, pepper and bamboo shoots to a stockpot and bring to a boil. Stir in the chicken and let cook for about 3-4 minutes.

In a small dish, make a slurry with the cornstarch and water. Add a bit at a time to the stockpot until the broth thickens to your desired consistency.

Stir in the beaten eggs and cook for about 45 seconds or until the eggs are done.

Remove from the heat and add the vinegar and tofu.

Garnish with sliced green onions.

Nutrition: Calories: 345 Fat: 1.2 g Carbs: 2.2 g Protein: 23.3 g Sodium: 145

PF Chang's Lettuce Wraps

Preparation Time: 10 minutes

Cooking Time: 10 minutes

Servings: 4

Ingredients:

1 tablespoon olive oil

1-pound ground chicken

2 cloves garlic, minced

1 onion, diced

¼ cup hoisin sauce

2 tablespoons soy sauce

1 tablespoon rice wine vinegar

1 tablespoon ginger, freshly grated

1 tablespoon Sriracha (optional)

1 (8-ounce) can whole water chestnuts, drained and diced

2 green onions, thinly sliced

Kosher salt and freshly ground black pepper to taste

1 head iceberg lettuce

Directions:

Add the oil to a deep skillet or saucepan and heat over medium-high heat. When hot, add the chicken and cook until it is completely cooked through. Stir while cooking to make sure it is properly crumbled.

Drain any excess fat from the skillet, then add the garlic, onion, hoisin sauce, soy sauce, ginger, sriracha and vinegar. Cook until the onions have softened, then stir in the water chestnuts and green onion and cook for another minute or so. Add salt and pepper to taste.

Serve with lettuce leaves and eat by wrapping them up like a taco.

Nutrition: Calories: 156 Fat: 4.3 g Carbs: 3.7 g Protein:27 g Sodium: 250 g

PF Chang's Shrimp Dumplings

Preparation Time: 20 minutes

Cooking Time: 10 minutes

Servings: 4-6

Ingredients:

1 pound medium shrimp, peeled, deveined, washed and dried, divided

2 tablespoons carrot, finely minced

2 tablespoons green onion, finely minced

1 teaspoon ginger, freshly minced

2 tablespoons oyster sauce

1/4 teaspoon sesame oil

1 package wonton wrappers

Sauce

1 cup soy sauce

2 tablespoons white vinegar

1/2 teaspoon chili paste

2 tablespoons granulated sugar

1/2 teaspoon ginger, freshly minced

Sesame oil to taste

1 cup water

1 tablespoon cilantro leaves

Directions:

In a food processor or blender, finely mince ½ pound of the shrimp.

Dice the other ½ pound of shrimp.

In a mixing bowl, combine both the minced and diced shrimp with the remaining ingredients.

Spoon about 1 teaspoon of the mixture into each wonton wrapper. Wet the edges of the wrapper with your finger, then fold up and seal tightly.

Cover and refrigerate for at least an hour.

In a medium bowl, combine all of the ingredients for the sauce and stir until well combined.

When ready to serve, boil water in a saucepan and cover with a steamer. You may want to lightly oil the steamer to keep the dumplings from sticking. Steam the dumplings for 7-10 minutes.

Serve with sauce.

Nutrition: Calories: 244 Fat: 20 g Carbs: 57 g Protein:63 g Sodium: 354 g

PF Chang's Spicy Chicken Noodle Soup

Preparation Time: 15 minutes

Cooking Time: 15 minutes

Servings: 4-6

Ingredients:

2 quarts chicken stock

1 tablespoon granulated sugar

3 tablespoons white vinegar

2 cloves garlic, minced

1 tablespoon ginger, freshly minced

¼ cup soy sauce

Sriracha sauce to taste

Red pepper flakes to taste

1-pound boneless chicken breast, cut into thin 2-3 inch pieces

3 tablespoons cornstarch

Salt to taste

1 cup mushrooms, sliced

1 cup grape tomatoes, halved

3 green onions, sliced

2 tablespoons fresh cilantro, chopped

½ pound pasta, cooked to just under package directions and drained

Directions:

Add the chicken stock, sugar, vinegar, garlic, ginger, soy sauce, Sriracha and red pepper flakes to a large saucepan. Bring to a boil, then lower the heat to a simmer. Let cook for 5 minutes.

Season chicken with salt to taste. In a resealable bag, combine the chicken and the cornstarch. Shake to coat.

Add the chicken to the simmering broth a piece at a time. Then add the mushrooms. Continue to cook for another 5 minutes.

Stir in the tomatoes, green onions, cilantro, and cooked pasta.

Serve with additional cilantro.

Nutrition: Calories: 100 Fat: 3.7 g Carbs: 6.7 g Protein: 48 g Sodium: 187 g

Pei Wei 's Thai Chicken Satay

Preparation Time: 20 minutes

Cooking Time: 10-20 minutes

Marinating Time: 20 minutes

Servings: 2-4

Ingredients:

1-pound boneless, skinless chicken thighs

6-inch bamboo skewers, soaked in water

Thai satay marinade

1 tablespoon coriander seeds

1 teaspoon cumin seeds

2 teaspoons chopped lemongrass

1 teaspoon salt

1 teaspoon turmeric powder

¼ teaspoon roasted chili

½ cup coconut milk

1½ tablespoons light brown sugar

1 teaspoon lime juice

2 teaspoons fish sauce

Peanut sauce

2 tablespoons soy sauce

1 tablespoon rice wine vinegar

2 tablespoons brown sugar

¼ cup peanut butter

1 teaspoon chipotle Tabasco

Whisk all ingredients until well incorporated. Store in an airtight container in the refrigerator. Will last for 3 days.

Thai sweet cucumber relish

¼ cup white vinegar

¾ cup sugar

¾ cup water

1 tablespoon ginger, minced

1 Thai red chili, minced

1 medium cucumber

1 tablespoon toasted peanuts, chopped

Directions:

Cut any excess fat from the chicken, then cut into strips about 3 inches long and 1 inch wide. Thread the strips onto the skewers.

Prepare the Thai Satay Marinade and the Peanut Sauce in separate bowls by simply whisking together all of the ingredients for each.

Dip the chicken skewers in the Thai Satay Marinade and allow to marinate for at least 4 hours. Reserve the marinade when you remove the chicken skewers.

You can either cook the skewers on the grill, basting with the marinade halfway through, or you can do the same in a 350-degree F oven. They taste better on the grill.

To prepare the Cucumber Relish, simply add all of the ingredients together and stir to make sure the cucumber is coated.

When the chicken skewers are done cooking, serve with peanut sauce and the cucumber relish.

Nutrition: Calories: 298 Fat: 5.4 g Carbs: 7.5 g Protein: 61g Sodium: 190 g

Pasta

Pesto Cavatappi from Noodles & Company

Preparation Time: 5 minutes

Cooking Time: 20 minutes

Servings: 80

Ingredients: 4 quarts water 1 tablespoon salt

1-pound macaroni pasta 1 teaspoon olive oil

1 large tomato, finely chopped

4-ounce mushrooms, finely chopped

¼ cup chicken broth ¼ cup dry white wine

¼ cup heavy cream 1 cup pesto

1 cup Parmesan cheese, grated

Directions:

Add water and salt to a pot. Bring to a boil. Put in pasta and cook for 10 minutes or until al dente. Drain and set aside.

In a pan, heat oil. Sauté tomatoes and mushrooms for 5 minutes. Pour in broth, wine, and cream. Bring to a boil. Reduce heat to medium and simmer for 2 minutes or until mixture is thick. Stir in pesto and cook for another 2 minutes. Toss in pasta. Mix until fully coated.

Transfer onto plates and sprinkle with Parmesan cheese.

Nutrition: Calories: 637 Fat: 42 g Carbs: 48 g Protein: 19 g Sodium: 1730 mg

Cajun Chicken Pasta from Chili's

Preparation Time: 10 minutes

Cooking Time: 20 minutes

Servings: 4

Ingredients:

2 chicken breasts, boneless and skinless

1 tablespoon olive oil, divided

1 tablespoon Cajun seasoning

3 quarts water

½ tablespoon salt

8 ounces penne pasta

2 tablespoons unsalted butter

3 garlic cloves, minced

1 cup heavy cream

½ teaspoon lemon zest

¼ cup Parmesan cheese, shredded

Salt and black pepper, to taste

1 tablespoon oil

2 Roma tomatoes, diced

2 tablespoons parsley chopped

Directions:

Place chicken in a Ziploc bag. Add 1 tablespoon oil and Cajun seasoning. Using your hands, combine chicken and mixture until well-coated. Seal tightly and set aside to marinate.

Cook pasta in a pot filled with salt and boiling water. Follow package instructions. Drain and set aside.

In a skillet, heat butter over medium heat. Sauté garlic for 1 minute or until aromatic. Slowly add cream, followed by lemon zest. Cook for 1 minute, stirring continuously until fully blended. Toss in Parmesan cheese. Mix until sauce is a little thick, then add salt and pepper. Add pasta and combine until well-coated. Transfer onto a bowl and keep warm.

In a separate skillet, heat remaining oil. Cook chicken over medium-high heat for about 5 minutes on each side or until fully cooked through. Transfer onto chopping board and cut into thin strips.

Top pasta with chicken and sprinkle with tomatoes and parsley on top.

Serve.

Nutrition: Calories: 655 Fat: 38 g Carbs: 47 g Protein: 31 g Sodium: 359 mg

Chow Mein from Panda Express

Preparation Time: 10 minutes

Cooking Time: 10 minutes

Servings: 4

Ingredients:

8 quarts water

12 ounces Yakisoba noodles

¼ cup soy sauce

3 garlic cloves, finely chopped

1 tablespoon brown sugar

2 teaspoons ginger, grated

¼ teaspoon white pepper, ground

2 tablespoons olive oil

1 onion, finely chopped

3 celery stalks, sliced on the bias

2 cups cabbage, chopped

Directions:

In a pot, bring water to a boil. Cook Yakisoba noodles for about 1 minute until noodles separate. Drain and set aside.

Combine soy sauce, garlic, brown sugar, ginger, and white pepper in a bowl.

In a pan, heat oil on medium-high heat. Sauté onion and celery for 3 minutes or until soft. Add cabbage and stir-fry for an additional minute. Mix in noodles and soy sauce mixture. Cook for 2 minutes, stirring continuously until noodles are well-coated.

Transfer into bowls. Serve.

Nutrition: Calories: 382 Fat: 8 g Carbs: 72 g Protein: 14 g Sodium: 1194 mg

Rattlesnake Pasta from Pizzeria Uno

Preparation Time: 5 minutes

Cooking Time: 25 minutes

Servings: 6

Ingredients:

Pasta:

4 quarts

1-pound penne pasta

1 dash of salt

Chicken:

2 tablespoons butter

2 cloves garlic, finely chopped

½ tablespoon Italian seasoning

1-pound chicken breast, boneless and skinless, cut into small squares

Sauce:

4 tablespoons butter

2 cloves garlic, finely chopped - ¼ cup all-purpose flour

1 tablespoon - salt ¾ teaspoon white pepper

2 cups milk - 1 cup half-and-half

¾ cup Parmesan cheese, shredded

8 ounces Colby cheese, shredded

3 jalapeno peppers, chopped

Directions:

In a pot of boiling water, add salt, and cook pasta according to package instructions. Drain well and set aside.

To prepare the chicken, heat butter in a pan. Sauté garlic and Italian seasoning for 1 minute. Add chicken and cook 5-7 minutes or until cooked thoroughly, flipping halfway through. Transfer onto a plate once. Set aside.

In the same pan, prepare the sauce. Add butter and heat until melted. Stir in garlic and cook for 30 seconds. Then, add flour, salt, and pepper. Cook for 2 more minutes, stirring continuously. Pour in milk and half-and-half. Keep stirring until sauce turns thick and smooth.

Toss in chicken, jalapeno peppers, and pasta. Stir until combined.

Serve.

Nutrition: Calories: 44 g Fat: 44 g Carbs: 72 g Protein: 40 g Sodium: 1791 mg

Copycat Kung Pao Spaghetti from California Pizza Kitchen

Preparation Time: 10 minutes

Cooking Time: 20 minutes

Servings: 4

Ingredients:

1-pound spaghetti

2 tablespoons vegetable oil

3 chicken breasts, boneless and skinless

Salt and pepper, to taste

4 garlic cloves, finely chopped

½ cup dry roasted peanuts

6 green onions, cut into half-inch pieces

10-12 Dried bird eyes hot peppers

Sauce:

½ cup soy sauce

½ cup chicken broth

½ cup dry sherry

2 tablespoons red chili paste with garlic

¼ cup sugar

2 tablespoons red wine vinegar

2 tablespoons cornstarch

1 tablespoon sesame oil

Directions:

Follow instructions on package to cook spaghetti noodles. Drain and set aside.

Add oil to a large pan over medium-high heat. Generously season chicken with salt and pepper, then add to pan once hot. Cook for about 3 to 4 minutes. Turn chicken over and cook for another 3 to 4 minutes. Remove from heat and allow to cool.

Mix together all sauce ingredients in a bowl.

Once chicken is cool enough to handle, chop chicken into small pieces. Set aside.

Return pan to heat. Add garlic and sauté for about 1 minute until aromatic. Pour in prepared sauce, then stir. Once boiling, lower heat and allow to simmer for about 1 to 2 minutes or until liquid thickens. Add pasta, cooked chicken, peanuts, hot peppers, and scallions. Mix well.

Serve.

Nutrition: Calories: 548 Fat: 22 g Saturated Fat: 7 g Carbs: 67 g Sugars: 16 g Fibers: 4 g Protein: 15 g Sodium: 2028 mg

Three Cheese Chicken Penne from Applebee's

Preparation Time: 10 minutes

Cooking Time: 1 hour

Servings: 4

Ingredients:

2 boneless skinless chicken breasts

1 cup Italian salad dressing

3 cups penne pasta

6 tablespoons olive oil, divided

15 ounces Alfredo sauce

8 ounces combination mozzarella, Parmesan, and provolone cheeses, grated

4 roma tomatoes, seeded and diced

4 tablespoons fresh basil, diced

2 cloves garlic, finely chopped

Shredded parmesan cheese for serving

Directions:

Preheat oven to 350°F.

In a bowl, add chicken then drizzle with Italian dressing. Mix to fully coat chicken with dressing. Cover using plastic wrap and keep inside refrigerator overnight but, if you're in a hurry, at least 2 hours is fine.

Follow instructions on package to cook penne pasta. Drain, then set aside.

Brush 3 tablespoons oil onto grates of grill then preheat to medium-high heat. Add marinated chicken onto grill, discarding the marinade. Cook chicken until both sides are fully cooked and internal temperature measures 165°F. Remove from grill. Set aside until cool enough to handle. Then, cut chicken into thin slices.

In a large bowl, add cooked noodles, Alfredo sauce, and grilled chicken. Mix until combined.

Drizzle remaining oil onto large casserole pan, then pour noodle mixture inside. Sprinkle cheeses on top. Bake for about 15-20 minutes or until cheese turns a golden and edges of mixture begins to bubble. Remove from oven.

Mix tomatoes, basil, and garlic in a bowl. Add on top of pasta.

Sprinkle parmesan cheese before serving.

Nutrition: Calories: 1402 Fat: 93 g Saturated fat: 27 g Carbs: 91 g Sugar: 7 g Fibers: 3 g Protein: 62 g Sodium: 5706 mg

Boston Market Mac n' Cheese

Preparation Time: 10 minutes

Cooking Time: 20 minutes

Servings: 8

Ingredients:

1 8-ounce package spiral pasta - 2 tablespoons butter

2 tablespoons all-purpose flour

1 ¾ cups whole milk

1 ¼ cups diced processed cheese like Velveeta™

¼ teaspoon dry mustard

½ teaspoon onion powder

1 teaspoon salt

Pepper, to taste

Directions:

Cook pasta according to package instructions. Drain, then set aside.

To prepare sauce make the roux with four and butter over medium-low heat in a large deep skillet. Add milk and whisk until well blended. Add cheese, mustard, salt, and pepper. Keep stirring until smooth.

Once pasta is cooked, transfer to a serving bowl. Pour cheese mixture on top. Toss to combine.

Serve warm.

Nutrition: Calories: 319 Fat: 17 g Saturated fat: 10 g Carbs: 28 g

Sugar: 7 g Fibers: 1 g Protein: 17 g Sodium: 1134 mg

Macaroni Grill's Pasta Milano

Preparation Time: 5 minutes

Cooking Time: 20 minutes

Servings: 6

Ingredients:

1 pound bowtie pasta

2 teaspoons olive oil

1 pound chicken, chopped into small pieces

1 12-ounce package mushrooms, chopped

1 cup onion, minced

2 garlic cloves, finely minced

½ cup sun dried tomatoes, diced

1½ cups half and half

1 tablespoon butter, softened

½ cup Parmesan cheese, shredded, plus some more for serving

1 teaspoon black pepper, ground

1 tablespoon fresh basil, minced

Directions:

Follow instructions on package to cook bowtie pasta. Drain, then set aside.

Add oil to a pan over medium-high heat. Once hot, add chicken and stir-fry for about 5 to 6 minutes until cooked through. Set chicken aside onto a plate.

In the same pan, toss in mushrooms, onions, garlic, and sundried tomatoes. Sauté until onions turn soft and mushrooms become a light brown, then sprinkle salt and pepper to season. Return chicken to pan and mix.

Mix half and half, butter, Parmesan, pepper, and basil in a small bowl.

Add half and half mixture to pan. Stir, and let simmer for about 3 to 4 minutes or until pan ingredients are thoroughly heated. Mix in pasta until coated well.

Serve.

Nutrition: Calories: 600 Fat: 18 g Saturated fat: 9 g Carbs: 69 g Sugar: 8 g Fibers: 5 g Protein: 42 g Sodium: 349 mg

Olive Garden's Fettuccine Alfredo

Preparation Time: 5 minutes

Cooking Time: 25 minutes

Servings: 6

Ingredients: ½ cup butter, melted

2 tablespoons cream cheese

1 pint heavy cream 1 teaspoon garlic powder

Some salt

Some black pepper

⅔ cup parmesan cheese, grated

1 pound fettuccine, cooked

Directions:

Melt the cream cheese in the melted butter over medium heat until soft.

Add the heavy cream and season the mixture with garlic powder, salt, and pepper.

Reduce the heat to low and allow the mixture to simmer for another 15 to 20 minutes.

Remove the mixture from heat and add in the parmesan. Stir everything to melt the cheese.

Pour the sauce over the pasta and serve.

Nutrition: Calories: 767.3 Fat: 52.9 g Carbs: 57.4 g Protein: 17.2 g Sodium: 367 mg

Red Lobster's Shrimp Pasta

Preparation Time: 5 minutes

Cooking Time: 30 minutes

Servings: 4

Ingredients:

8 ounces linguini or spaghetti pasta

⅓ cup extra virgin olive oil

3 garlic cloves

1 pound shrimp, peeled, deveined

⅔ cup clam juice or chicken broth

⅓ cup white wine

1 cup heavy cream

½ cup parmesan cheese, freshly grated

¼ teaspoon dried basil, crushed

¼ teaspoon dried oregano, crushed

Fresh parsley and parmesan cheese for garnish

Directions:

Cook the Pasta according to package directions.

Simmer the garlic in hot oil over low heat, until tender.

Increase the heat to low to medium and add the shrimp. When the shrimp is cooked, transfer it to a separate bowl along with the garlic. Keep the remaining oil in the pan.

Pour the clam or chicken broth into the pan and bring to a boil.

Add the wine and adjust the heat to medium. Keep cooking the mixture for another 3 minutes.

While stirring the mixture, reduce the heat to low and add in the cream and cheese. Keep stirring.

When the mixture thickens, return the shrimp to the pan and throw in the remaining ingredients (except the pasta).

Place the pasta in a bowl and pour the sauce over it.

Mix everything together and serve. Garnish with parsley and parmesan cheese, if desired

Nutrition: Calories: 590 Fat: 26 g Carbs: 54 g Protein: 34 g Sodium: 1500 mg

+ Cheesecake Factory's Cajun Jambalaya Pasta

Preparation Time: 10 minutes

Cooking Time: 40 minutes

Servings: 4

Ingredients:

Cajun Seasoning Blend:

1 teaspoon white pepper

1 teaspoon cayenne pepper

3 teaspoons salt

1 teaspoon paprika

½ teaspoon garlic powder

½ teaspoon onion powder

Chicken and Shrimp:

2 boneless skinless chicken breasts, halved, cut into bite-size pieces

½ pound large shrimp, peeled, deveined

1 tablespoon olive oil

Pasta:

5 quarts water

6 ounces fettuccine

6 ounces spinach fettuccine

Jambalaya:

1 tablespoon olive oil

2 medium tomatoes, chopped

1 medium onion, sliced

1 green bell pepper, sliced

1 red bell pepper, sliced

1 yellow bell pepper, sliced

1½ cups chicken stock

1 tablespoon cornstarch

2 tablespoons white wine

2 teaspoons arrowroot powder

2 teaspoons fresh parsley, chopped

Directions:

Mix all of the Cajun seasoning blend ingredients together to make the seasoning. Divide the seasoning into 3 equal parts.

Coat the chicken and shrimp with ⅓ of the seasoning each.

Cook pasta according to package directions.

While waiting for the pasta, sauté the spiced chicken in heated oil in a large skillet.

When the chicken starts turning brown, stir in the shrimp and cook until the chicken is cooked tough and shrimp turn pink.

Transfer the chicken and shrimp to a plate and set aside.

Using the same pan, warm the oil for the jambalaya over medium heat. Add the tomatoes, onions, peppers, and remaining 1/3 of the seasoning mix. Sauté for 10 minutes.

When the vegetables turn brownish-black, add the chicken and shrimp back to the mix.

Pour in ¾ cup of the chicken stock to deglaze the pan. Gently scrape the pan to remove the burnt particles. Turn the heat to high and allow the mixture to cook.

When the broth has evaporated completely, add in the remaining stock and cook for another 5 minutes.

Turn the heat down to low and leave the mixture to rest over heat. In a bowl, mix the white wine and arrowroot until it dissolves.

Add the mixture to the jambalaya. Turn the heat to low and leave the mixture to simmer.

When the jambalaya and pasta are done, assemble the dish by:

a)   Putting the pasta as the first layer;

b)   Covering the pasta with the jambalaya sauce; and

c)   Garnish each plate with parsley.

Nutrition: Calories: 563.9 Fat: 13.3 g Carbs: 73.8 g Protein: 35.9 g Sodium: 1457.6 mg

Olive Garden's Steak Gorgonzola

Preparation Time: 10 minutes

Cooking Time: 1 hour and 30 minutes

Servings: 6

Ingredients:

Pasta:

2½ pounds boneless beef top sirloin steaks, cut into ½-inch cubes

1 pound fettucine or linguini, cooked

2 tablespoons sun-dried tomatoes, chopped

2 tablespoons balsamic vinegar glaze

Some fresh parsley leaves, chopped

Marinade:

1½ cups Italian dressing

1 tablespoon fresh rosemary, chopped

1 tablespoon fresh lemon juice (optional)

Spinach Gorgonzola Sauce:

4 cups baby spinach, trimmed

2 cups Alfredo sauce (recipe follows)

½ cup green onion, chopped

6 tablespoons gorgonzola, crumbled, and divided)

Directions:

Cook the pasta and set aside. Mix together the marinade ingredients in a sealable container.

Marinate the beef in the container for an hour.

While the beef is marinating, make the Spinach Gorgonzola sauce. Heat the Alfredo sauce in a saucepan over medium heat. Add spinach and green onions. Let simmer until the spinach wilt. Crumble 4 tablespoons of the Gorgonzola cheese on top of the sauce. Let melt and stir. Set aside remaining 2 tablespoons of the cheese for garnish. Set aside and cover with lid to keep warm.

When the beef is done marinating, grill each piece depending on your preference.

Toss the cooked pasta and the Alfredo sauce in a saucepan, and then transfer to a plate.

Top the pasta with the beef, and garnish with balsamic glaze, sun-dried tomatoes, crumble gorgonzola cheese, and parsley leaves.

Serve and enjoy.

Nutrition: Calories: 740.5 Fat: 27.7 g Carbs: 66 g Protein: 54.3 g Sodium: 848.1 mg

+ Noodles and Company's Pad Thai

Preparation Time: 5 minutes

Cooking Time: 20 minutes

Servings: 4

Ingredients:

Sauce:

½ cup boiling water

¼ cup brown sugar

6 tablespoons lime juice

¼ cup rice vinegar

¼ cup Thai fish sauce

2 teaspoons Sriracha

Pad Thai:

12 ounces fettuccine or linguine (uncooked)

2 tablespoons canola oil, divided

½ yellow onion, sliced

3 cloves fresh garlic. pressed or minced

3 eggs, lightly beaten

½ cup cabbage, sliced

½ cup mushrooms, sliced

1 cup carrots, sliced

1 cup broccoli, chopped

Garnish: cilantro, sliced green onions, lime wedges

Directions:

Dissolve the sugar in the boiling water. When the sugar has completely dissolved, mix in the lime juice, vinegar, fish sauce, and Sriracha.

Cook the noodles.

Sauté the onion in 1 tablespoon of oil over medium to high heat for 1 minute. Add in the garlic and sauté for another 30 seconds. Mix the eggs into the garlic and onion mixture, and continue to cook until the egg is cooked completely.

Transfer the egg mixture to a bowl and add the remaining oil to the same pan. Sauté the vegetables.

When the vegetables are crispy, add in half of the sauce and cook for 1 to 3 minutes. When your desired consistency is reached, add in the egg mixture and noodles and transfer to a plate to serve.

Nutrition: Calories: 830 Fat: 18 g Carbs: 151 g Protein: 15 g Sodium: 1300 mg

Cheesecake Factory's Pasta di Vinci

Preparation Time: 10 minutes

Cooking Time: 50 minutes

Servings: 4

Ingredients:

½ red onion, chopped

1 cup mushrooms, quartered

2 teaspoons garlic, chopped

1 pound chicken breast, cut into bite-size pieces

3 tablespoons butter, divided

2 tablespoons flour

2 teaspoons salt

¼ cup white wine

1 cup cream of chicken soup mixed with some milk

4 tablespoons heavy cream

Basil leaves for serving, chopped

Parmesan cheese for serving

1 pound penne pasta, cooked, drained

Directions:

Sauté the onion, mushrooms and garlic in 1 tablespoon of the butter.

When they are tender, remove them from the butter and place in a bowl. Cook the chicken in the same pan.

When the chicken is done, transfer it to the bowl containing the garlic, onions, and mushrooms, and set everything aside.

Using the same pan, make a roux using the flour and remaining butter over low to medium heat. When the roux is ready, mix in the salt, wine, and cream of chicken mixture. Continue stirring the mixture, making sure that it does not burn.

When the mixture thickens and allow the mixture to simmer for a few more minutes.

Mix in the ingredients that you set aside, and transfer the cooked pasta to a bowl or plate.

Pour the sauce over the pasta, garnish with parmesan cheese and basil, and serve.

Nutrition: Calories: 844.9 Fat: 35.8 g Carbs: 96.5 g Protein: 33.9 g Sodium: 1400.2 mg

Longhorn Steakhouse's Mac & Cheese

Preparation Time: 20 minutes

Cooking Time: 20 minutes

Servings: 10

Ingredients:

1 pound cavatappi pasta, cooked

2 tablespoons butter

2 tablespoons flour

2 cups half-and-half

2 ounces gruyere cheese, shredded

8 ounces white cheddar, shredded

2 tablespoons parmesan cheese, shredded

4 ounces fontina cheese, shredded

1 teaspoon smoked paprika

4 pieces bacon, crispy, crumbled

½ cup panko bread crumbs

Directions:

Make a roux by cooking the melted butter and flour over medium heat.

When the roux is cooked, add in the half-and-half ½ cup at a time, adding more as the sauce thickens.

Slowly add the rest of the ingredients (except the pasta) one at a time, really allowing each ingredient to incorporate itself into the sauce. Continue stirring the mixture until everything is heated.

Place the pasta in a greased 13×9 baking pan or 6 individual baking dishes and pour the sauce over it. Sprinkle the bacon and panko bread crumbs over the top of the pasta.

Bake the pasta in an oven preheated to 350°F for 20-25 minutes, or until breadcrumbs start to become golden brown.

Let the pasta cool, and serve.

Nutrition: Calories: 610 Fat: 37 g Carbs: 43 g Protein: 26 g Sodium: 1210 mg

Soups and Side Dishes

Breadsticks

Preparation Time: 60 minutes

Cooking Time: 15 minutes

Servings: 16

Ingredients:

Breadsticks

1½ cups warm water

2 tablespoons sugar

1 packet (1 tablespoon/¾ ounce) yeast

2 teaspoons fine sea salt (and a bit extra to sprinkle on top)

2 tablespoons butter, softened

4-5 cups bread flour (you can also use all-purpose flour, but the breadsticks will turn out denser)

Topping

¼ cup butter

1 teaspoon garlic powder

Directions:

To make the breadsticks, combine the warm water, sugar, and yeast in a large bowl.

Proof for 10 minutes. Mix in the salt, softened butter, and 3 cups of bread flour.

Mix in the rest of the bread flour to get a soft dough.

Cover the bowl with a damp towel and set aside in a warm place. Let dough rise for 1 hour.

Gently knead the dough and separate into 14-16 balls.

Roll each ball into a log of your desired length. Place on two cookie sheets and let rise for 15-30 minutes.

To make the topping, melt the butter and mix with the garlic powder.

Brush the topping mixture over the breadsticks and finish with sprinkles of sea salt.

Bake at 400°F for 12-14 minutes.

Brush the remaining garlic butter on top of the breadsticks.

Nutrition: Calories: 156 Fat: 67 g Carbs: 98. 7 g Protein: 34 .9 g Sodium: 756 mg

Chicken Gnocchi Soup

Preparation Time: 10 minutes

Cooking Time: 8 minutes

Servings: 4

Ingredients:

1 tablespoon oil

1½ pounds chicken breast, cubed

½ cup celery, chopped

½ cup onion, chopped

2 cups chicken broth

1 cup matchstick carrots

1 teaspoon thyme

3 cups half and half

1 (16-ounce) package gnocchi

2 cups fresh spinach

Directions:

Place oil, chicken, and celery in the Instant Pot. Sauté until meat is brown.

Mix in chicken broth, carrots, and thyme. Close the lid and the pressure release valve.

Set to Manual, High Pressure for 4 minutes. Once completed, quick release pressure.

Open the lid and set to sauté. Add spinach, half and half and gnocchi. Leave Instant Pot on sauté to heat the soup until it is boiling.

Let boil and keep stirring for 3 minutes or until gnocchi is cooked. Serve.

Nutrition: Calories: 237 Fat: 45 g Carbs: 12. 7 g Protein: 45. 6 g Sodium: 458 mg

Zuppa Toscana

Preparation Time: 20 minutes

Cooking Time: 4 hours

Servings: 8

Ingredients:

1 pound ground hot Italian sausage

1 tablespoon garlic, minced

1 yellow onion, chopped

4 russet potatoes, diced

1 quart chicken broth

1 bunch kale

¾ cup heavy whipping cream

¼ cup parmesan, shredded

Directions:

In a large skillet, crumble the Italian sausage and cook on medium-high heat for about 5-8 minutes.

Add the onions and garlic and cook for about 2-3 minutes.

Drain the grease and move the cooked sausages and veggies to a 6-quart crock pot (or larger). Add the diced potatoes and season with salt and pepper.

Pour in enough chicken broth to cover the potatoes. Add up to 2 cups of water if there isn't enough chicken broth.

Stir, then cover. Set to cook on low for 5-6 hours or high for 3-4 hours.

Add the kale and heavy whipping cream. Stir

Replace the cover and let cook for another 30 minutes on high. Serve topped with parmesan cheese.

Nutrition: Calories: 345 Fat: 87 g Carbs: 83. 9 g Protein: 69. 2 g Sodium: 837 mg

Minestrone

Preparation Time: 15 minutes

Cooking Time: 1 hour and 20 minutes

Servings: 6 to 8

Ingredients:

3 tablespoons olive oil

1 medium onion, diced

1 small zucchini, chopped

1 (14-ounce) can Italian-style green beans

1 stalk celery, diced

4 teaspoons garlic, minced

1 quart vegetable broth

2 (15-ounce) cans red kidney beans, drained

2 (15-ounce) cans great northern beans, drained

1 (14-ounce) can diced tomatoes with juice

½ cup carrot, shredded

½ cup dry red wine (optional) ½ cup tomato paste

1 teaspoon oregano   1 teaspoon basil

¼ teaspoon thyme

½ teaspoon garlic powder

½ teaspoon onion powder   1 bay leaf

3 cups hot water

4 cups fresh spinach

1½ cups shell pasta

Salt and pepper to taste

Directions:

In a large stockpot, heat olive oil and sauté onion, celery, zucchini and carrots over medium heat.

Stir in garlic, green beans, and tomato paste. Then add broth, red wine, hot water, tomatoes, green beans, oregano, basil, thyme, garlic powder, onion powder, and bay leaf.

Bring soup to a boil. Reduce heat, cover and simmer for 45 minutes. Remove bay leaf.

Mix in spinach and pasta. Cook for 30 minutes. Serve.

Nutrition: Calories: 265 Fat: 45 g Carbs: 32.4 g Protein: 54.8 g Sodium: 3457 mg

House Salad and Dressing

Preparation Time: 10 minutes

Cooking Time: 0

Servings: 12

Ingredients:

Salad

1 head iceberg lettuce

¼ small red onion, sliced thin

6–12 black olives, pitted

6 pepperoncini

2 small roma tomatoes, sliced

Croutons

¼ cup shredded or grated romano or parmesan cheese

Dressing

1 packet Italian dressing mix

¾ cup vegetable/canola oil

¼ cup olive oil

1 tablespoon mayonnaise

⅓ cup white vinegar

¼ cup water

½ teaspoon sugar

½ teaspoon dried Italian seasoning

½ teaspoon salt

¼ teaspoon pepper

¼ teaspoon garlic powder

Directions:

To make the dressing, combine all ingredients in a small bowl. Thoroughly whisk together. Refrigerate for 1 hour to marinate.

Add the salad ingredient to a salad bowl. When ready to serve, add some of the dressing to the salad and toss to coat. Add grated cheese as a garnish as desired.

Store remaining dressing in an airtight container. Keep refrigerated and it can be stored for up to 3 weeks.

Nutrition: Calories: 435 Fat: 54. 8 g Carbs: 46.4 g Protein: 13.9 g Sodium: 5675 mg

Santa Fe Crispers Salad

Preparation Time: 10 minutes

Cooking Time: 30 minutes

Servings: 4

Ingredients: 1 ½ pounds boneless skinless chicken breasts

1 tablespoon fresh cilantro, chopped

¾ cup Lawry's Santa Fe Chili Marinated with Lime and Garlic, divided

1 package (10 ounces) torn romaine lettuce, approximately 8 cups

2 tablespoons milk   1 cup black beans, drained and rinsed

½ cup sour cream   1 cup drained canned whole kernel corn

¼ cup red onion, chopped

1 medium avocado, cut into chunks

½ cup Monterey Jack, shredded

1 medium tomato, cut into chunks

Directions:

Place chicken in a large glass dish or re-sealable marinade plastic bag

Add approximately ½ cup of the Santa Fe marinade, turn several times until nicely coated

Refrigerate for 30 minutes or longer

Removed the chicken from marinade; get rid of the leftover marinade

Grill the chicken until cooked through, for 6 to 7 minutes per side, over medium heat; brushing with 2 tablespoons of the leftover marinade

Cut the chicken into thin slices.

Combine the sour cream together with milk, leftover marinade and cilantro with wire whisk in medium-sized bowl until smooth

Arrange lettuce on large serving platter

Top with the chicken, avocado, corn, beans, cheese, tomato and onion.

Serve with tortilla chips and dressing. Enjoy.

Nutrition: Calories: 676 Fat: 86 g Carbs: 67 g Protein: 46 g Sodium: 2434 mg

Quesadilla Explosion Salad

Preparation Time: 20 minutes

Cooking Time: 20 minutes

Servings: 1

Ingredients:

1 vegetarian chicken patty

6 ounces bagged salad mix

For Chipotle Ranch Dressing:

1 cup 2% milk

1 packet ranch dressing mix

1 teaspoon chipotle peppers in adobo sauce

1 cup non-fat Greek yogurt

For Citrus Balsamic Vinaigrette

2 tablespoon balsamic vinegar

½ teaspoon orange zest

2 tablespoon Splenda

¼ cup orange juice

A pinch of nutmeg

For Sweet Potato Strips:

¼ medium sweet potato, washed, thinly sliced & cut into strips nonstick cooking spray

¼ teaspoon salt

For Cheese Quesadilla:

1 mission carb balance whole wheat fajita sized tortilla

1 ounce reduced-fat Colby jack cheese, shredded

For Roasted Corn and Black Bean Salsa:

1 cup black beans, rinsed

2 ears of corn, roasted, kernels removed from cob

½ cup fresh cilantro, chopped

1 tablespoon lime juice, freshly squeezed

¼ red onion, chopped

1 jalapeno pepper, roasted, peeled, seeded, de-veined & chopped

Salt to taste

1 red bell pepper, medium, roasted, peeled, seeded & chopped

Directions:

For Sweet Potato Strips:

Preheat oven to 350 F. Lightly coat the strips with nonstick cooking spray and then, dust them lightly with the salt. Place on a large-sized cookie sheet in a single layer & bake for 15 to 20 minutes. Don't forget to stir the strips & turn halfway during the baking process.

Set aside and let cool until ready to use.

For Roasted Corn Salsa:

Add corn together with peppers & black beans to a large bowl and then squeeze the lime juice on top; add salt to taste. Give the ingredients a good stir & add the fresh cilantro.

For Chipotle Ranch Dressing:

Add yogurt and milk to the ranch dressing mix. Stir in the chipotle & store in a refrigerator.

For Citrus Balsamic Vinaigrette:

Over low heat in a large saucepan; place the entire ingredients together & cook for a minute. Set aside and let cool then refrigerate.

For Quesadilla:

1.Place the cheese on half of the tortilla & then fold over.

Lightly coat the tortilla with the nonstick cooking spray & then cook over medium-high heat in a large pan. Cook until the cheese is completely melted, for a minute per side. Cut into 4 wedges.

Prepare the veggie "chicken" patty as per the directions mentioned on the package & then slice into thin strips.

Place approximately 6 ounces of the salad mix on the plate and then top with the "chicken" strips, black bean salsa, sweet potato strips & roasted corn.

Place the cut quesadilla around the edge of the plate and then drizzle the salad with the prepared dressings.

Nutrition: Calories: 245 Fat: 59.8 g Carbs: 67.3 g Protein: 12. 8 g Sodium: 4354 mg

Caribbean Shrimp Salad

Preparation Time: 20 minutes

Cooking Time: 55 minutes

Servings: 4

Ingredients:

8 cups baby spinach, fresh

¼ cup lime juice, freshly squeezed

2 tablespoons chili garlic sauce

½ teaspoon paprika

4 cups cooked shrimp, chopped (approximately 1 ½ pounds)

1 tablespoon grated lime rind

5 tablespoons seasoned rice vinegar, divided

½ teaspoon ground cumin

1 cup peeled mango, chopped

½ cup green onions, thinly sliced

2 garlic cloves, minced

1 cup radishes, julienne-cut

¼ cup peeled avocado, diced

2 tablespoons pumpkinseed kernels, unsalted

1 ½ tablespoons olive oil

Dash of salt

Directions:

In a large bowl; combine the cooked shrimp together with chili garlic sauce & 2 tablespoons of vinegar; toss well. Cover & let chill for an hour.

Now, in a small bowl; combine the leftover vinegar together with garlic cloves, oil, lime juice, lime rind, ground cumin, paprika & salt; stirring well with a whisk.

Place 2 cups of spinach on each of 4 plates; top each serving with a cup of the prepared shrimp mixture. Arrange ¼ cup radishes, ¼ cup mango & 1 tablespoon of the avocado around the shrimp on each plate. Top each serving with approximately 1 ½ teaspoons of pumpkinseed kernels & 2 tablespoons of green onions. Drizzle each salad with approximately 2 tablespoons of the vinaigrette. Serve and enjoy.

Nutrition: Calories: 124 Fat: 76.9 g Carbs: 67. 9 g Protein: 45. 8 g Sodium: 568 mg

Southwest Caesar Salad

Preparation Time: 10 minutes

Cooking Time: 20 minutes

Servings: 6

Ingredients:

2 tablespoon mayonnaise

¼ teaspoon cayenne or ground red pepper

6 cups fresh romaine lettuce, washed, shredded (approximately 1 head)

⅓ cup parmesan cheese, grated

1 cup croutons

½ of a red bell pepper, cut into thin strips

1 cup whole kernel corn, frozen & thawed

½ cup fresh cilantro, chopped

2 tablespoon green onion, chopped

¼ cup olive oil

2 tablespoon lime juice, freshly squeezed

1/8 teaspoon salt

Directions:

Place onions together with mayo, ground red pepper, lime juice and salt in a blender or food processor; cover & process until blended well. Slowly add the oil at top using the feed tube & continue to process after each addition until blended well.

Toss the lettuce with the corn, croutons, bell peppers, cheese and cilantro in a large bowl.

Add the mayo mixture; evenly toss until nicely coated. Serve immediately & enjoy.

Nutrition: Calories: 265 Fat: 62 g Carbs: 98 g Protein: 47 g Sodium:467 mg

Chili's Chili

Preparation Time: 10 minutes

Cooking Time: 1 hour and 10 minutes

Servings: 8

Ingredients:

For Chili:

4 pounds ground chuck - ground for chili

1 ½ cups yellow onions, chopped

16 ounces tomato sauce

1 tablespoon cooking oil

3 ¼ plus 1 cups water

1 tablespoon masa harina

For Chili Spice Blend:

1 tablespoon paprika

½ cup chili powder

1 teaspoon ground black pepper

1/8 cup ground cumin

1 teaspoon cayenne pepper or to taste

1/8 cup salt

1 teaspoon garlic powder

Directions:

Combine the entire chili spice ingredients together in a small bowl; continue to combine until thoroughly mixed.

Now, over moderate heat in a 6-quart stock pot; place & cook the meat until browned; drain. In the meantime; combine the chili spice mix together with tomato sauce & 3 ¼ cups of water in the bowl; give the ingredients a good stir until blended well.

Add the chili seasoning liquid to the browned meat; give it a good stir & bring the mixture to a boil over moderate heat.

Over medium heat in a large skillet; heat 1 tablespoon of the cooking oil & sauté the onions until translucent, for a couple of minutes. Add the sautéed onions to the chili.

Decrease the heat to low & let simmer for an hour, stirring after every 10 to 15 minutes. Combine the masa harina with the leftover water in a separate bowl; mix well. Add to the chili stock pot & cook for 10 more minutes.

Nutrition: Calories: 143 Fat: 51. 3 g Carbs: 63.6 g Protein: 13.8 g Sodium: 1367 mg

Chicken Enchilada Soup

Preparation Time: 10 minutes

Cooking Time: 15 minutes

Servings: 10

Ingredients:

2 rotisserie chickens or 3 pounds cooked diced chicken

½ pound processed American cheese; cut in small cubes

3 cups yellow onions, diced

¼ cup chicken base

2 cups masa harina

½ teaspoon cayenne pepper

2 teaspoon granulated garlic

1 - 2 teaspoons salt or to taste

2 cups tomatoes, crushed

½ cup vegetable oil

2 teaspoon chili powder

4 quarts water

2 teaspoon ground cumin

Directions:

Over moderate heat in a large pot; combine oil together with onions, chicken base, granulated garlic, chili powder, cumin, cayenne & salt. Cook for 3 to 5 minutes, until onions are soft & turn translucent, stirring occasionally.

Combine 1 quart of water with masa harina in a large measuring cup or pitcher.

Continue to stir until no lumps remain. Add to the onions; bring the mixture to a boil, over moderate heat.

Once done, cook for a couple of minutes, stirring constantly. Stir in the tomatoes & leftover 3 quarts of water. Bring the soup to a boil again, stirring every now and then. Add in the cheese.

Cook until the cheese is completely melted, stirring occasionally. Add the chicken & cook until heated through. Serve immediately & enjoy.

Nutrition: Calories: 356 Fat: 53.9 g Carbs: 25. 6 g Protein: 12.8 g Sodium: 454 mg

Chicken Mushroom Soup

Preparation Time: 10 minutes

Cooking Time: 4 hours and 10 minutes

Servings: 4

Ingredients:

½ cup All-purpose flour

5 boneless & skinless chicken breasts, cubed

½ small onion, diced

3 cups mushrooms, sliced

¼ cup carrots, diced

6 cups chicken Broth

¼ cup softened butter, at room temperature

3 cups heavy cream

½ teaspoon white pepper

1 teaspoon lemon juice, freshly squeezed

¼ teaspoon dried thyme

Ground black pepper & kosher salt, to taste

⅛ teaspoon dried tarragon

Directions:

Over medium heat in a large pot; heat the butter until completely melted and then toss in the onion, chicken, mushrooms & carrots. Sauté until the chicken is cooked through; cover the ingredients with the all-purpose flour.

Pour in the chicken broth, white pepper, thyme, tarragon, pepper & salt. Bring the mixture to a simmer & cook for 10 to 12 minutes.

Add the lemon juice and heavy cream. Let simmer again for 10 to 12 more minutes.

Serve hot & enjoy.

Nutrition: Calories: 146 Fat: 16.9 g Carbs: 25.8 Protein: 41 g Sodium: 215 mg

Carrabba's Sausage and Lentil Soup

Preparation Time: 10 minutes

Cooking Time: 1 hour 5 minutes

Servings: 6

Ingredients:

1 pound Italian sausages

1 large onion, diced

1 stalk celery, diced

2 large carrots, diced

1 small zucchini, diced

6 cups low sodium chicken broth

2 cans (14.5 ounces each) tomatoes, diced, with juice

2 cups dry lentils

2-3 garlic cloves, minced

1 ½ teaspoons salt

1 teaspoon black pepper

1-3 pinches red pepper flakes, more if you like it spicier

1 teaspoon dry basil

½ teaspoon dry oregano

½ teaspoon parsley

½ teaspoon dry thyme

Parmesan cheese for garnishing

Directions:

Preheat the oven to 350°F. Place sausages on a baking dish and poke a few holes in each sausage with a fork. Bake for 20-30 minutes, or until the sausages are done. Let cool down and slice the sausages.

Chop and mince the ingredients as specified in the ingredients list.

Place all the ingredients, except the parmesan cheese, in a large pot.

Bring the soup to a boil, then lower the heat and cover the pot.

Let the mixture simmer for an hour, adding water to reduce thickness when necessary. If you want a thicker soup, puree a portion of the soup and return it.

Ladle the soup into bowls and garnish with parmesan cheese before serving

Nutrition: Calories: 221 Fat: 10 g Carbs: 20 g Protein: 13 g Sodium: 1182 mg

Compilation of Famous Main Dishes I

Bistro Shrimp Pasta

Preparation Time: 30 minutes

Cooking Time: 45 minutes

Servings: 8

Ingredients:

2 tablespoons olive oil

1 cup button mushrooms, quartered

1 cup grape tomatoes, halved

1 pound thin spaghetti, cooked

For the Lemon Basil Cream Sauce

¼ cup butter

4 garlic cloves, minced

2 cups heavy whipping cream

2 cups chicken broth

½ cup lemon juice

¼ cup cornstarch

½ teaspoon pepper

1 cup chopped fresh basil

For the shrimp

1 pound raw shrimp, deveined and with shells removed

2 eggs, beaten

1 cup flour

1 cup panko

1 teaspoon garlic powder

1 teaspoon Italian seasoning

3 tablespoons butter

Directions:

In a small skillet, cook the mushrooms in 2 tablespoons of olive oil. When they are soft, stir in the tomatoes and set the skillet aside.

Make the cream sauce: in a large skillet, melt the butter. Add the garlic and cook until fragrant. Pour in the cream and chicken broth, and bring to a low boil. Reduce the heat and let the sauce cook until the liquid reduces by half.

In a small dish, whisk the corn starch into the lemon juice, mixing until it is smooth and free of lumps, making slurry. Add the slurry into the chicken broth mixture.

To make the shrimp, beat the eggs in one small dish and combine the panko, flour, garlic powder, and Italian seasoning in a different one. Then dip each shrimp in the egg mixture and then into the panko.

Using the skillet you cooked the mushroom and tomatoes in, melt the 3 tablespoons of butter. When the shrimp turns nicely golden, remove it from skillet and let it drain on a plated lined with paper towel.

Add the fresh basil to the sauce and stir.

To serve, put some pasta on the plate, cover with sauce, and top with shrimp.

Nutrition: Calories: 234 Fat: 16 g Carbs: 81.9 g Protein: 76. 7 g Sodium: 656 mg

Crispy Crab Wontons

Preparation Time: 10 minutes

Cooking Time: 15 minutes

Servings: 4

Ingredients:

4 ounces cream cheese

2 tablespoons sweet and sour chili sauce (plus more for serving)

1 ½ teaspoons mustard

1 teaspoon chili garlic paste

1 teaspoon lemon juice

½ teaspoon granulated sugar

4 ounces crab meat

2 ounces sliced water chestnuts, minced

2 tablespoons green onions, finely chopped

1 ounce mozzarella cheese, grated

1 ounce fontina cheese, grated

¼ cup panko breadcrumbs

25 small square wonton wrappers, approximately 3-½ inches

Oil for frying

Directions:

In a large bowl, mix together the cream cheese, sweet and sour sauce, mustard, garlic paste, lemon juice, and sugar. Stir until well combined, then gently add in the crab, the water chestnuts, and green onions.

In a separate bowl, combine the mozzarella, fontina, and panko breadcrumbs. Carefully fold them into the cream cheese mixture, until well distributed.

Heat enough oil in a large skillet or saucepan so that the wontons won't touch the bottom when you cook them.

Lay out a wonton wrapper and fill it with about a teaspoon of filling. Pinch the sides of the wonton up and seal with a bit of water on your fingers.

When the oil is about 350°F, fry the wontons until they turn a golden brown. Transfer them to a plate lined with paper towel to drain.

Serve the wontons with sweet and sour chili sauce.

Nutrition: Calories: 724 Fat: 39 g Carbs: 89 g Protein: 65 g Sodium: 1587 mg

Chicken Casserole

Preparation Time: 10 minutes

Cooking Time: 1 hour and 20 minutes

Servings: 4

Ingredients:

Crust

1 cup yellow cornmeal

⅓ cup all-purpose flour

1½ teaspoons baking powder

1 tablespoon sugar

½ teaspoon salt

½ teaspoon baking soda

2 tablespoons vegetable oil

¾ cup buttermilk

1 egg

Filling

2½ cups cooked chicken breast, cut into bite sized pieces

¼ cup chopped yellow onion

½ cup sliced celery

1 teaspoon salt

¼ teaspoon ground pepper

1 (10.5-ounce) can condensed cream of chicken soup

1¾ cups chicken broth

2 tablespoons butter

½ cup melted butter

Directions:

Preheat the oven to 375°F.

To make the crust, in a large bowl, combine all of the crust ingredients until smooth.

Dump this mixture into a buttered or greased 8×8-inch baking dish. Bake for about 20 minutes, then remove from oven and allow to cool. Reduce oven temperature to 350°F.

Crumble the cooled cornbread mixture. Add to a large mixing bowl along with ½ cup of melted butter. Set aside.

Make the chicken filling by adding the butter to a large saucepan over medium heat. Let it melt, then add the celery and onions and cook until soft.

Add the chicken broth, cream of chicken soup, salt and pepper. Stir until everything is well combined. Add the cooked chicken breast pieces and stir again. Cook for 5 minutes at a low simmer.

Transfer the filling mixture into 4 individual greased baking dishes or into a greased casserole dish. Top with the cornbread mixture and transfer to the oven.

Bake for 35-40 minutes for a large casserole dish or 25-30 minutes for individual dishes.

Nutrition: Calories: 454 Fat: 65 g Carbs: 98 g Protein: 88 g Sodium: 387 mg

Sunday Chicken

Preparation Time: 10 minutes

Cooking Time: 10 minutes

Servings: 4

Ingredients:

Oil for frying

4 boneless, skinless chicken breasts

1 cups all-purpose flour

1 cup bread crumbs

2 teaspoons salt

2 teaspoons black pepper

1 cup buttermilk

½ cup water

Directions:

Add 3-4 inches of oil to a large pot or a deep fryer and preheat to 350°F.

Mix together the flour, breadcrumbs, salt and pepper in a shallow dish. To a separate shallow dish, add the buttermilk and water; stir.

Pound the chicken breasts to a consistent size. Dry them with a paper towel, then sprinkle with salt and pepper.

Dip the seasoned breasts in the flour mixture, then the buttermilk mixture, then back into the flour.

Add the breaded chicken to the hot oil and fry for about 8 minutes. Turn the chicken as necessary so that it cooks evenly on both sides.

Remove the chicken to either a wire rack or a plate lined with paper towels to drain.

Serve with mashed potatoes or whatever sides you love.

Nutrition: Calories:265 Fat: 47.9 g Carbs: 65. 5 g Protein: 37. 4 g

Sodium: 454 mg

Creamy Chicken and Rice

Preparation Time: 10 minutes

Cooking Time: 45 minutes

Servings: 4

Ingredients:

Salt and pepper to taste

2 cups cooked rice

1 diced onion

1 can cream of mushroom soup

1 packet chicken gravy

1½ pounds chicken breasts, cut into strips

Directions:

Preheat the oven to 350°F.

Cook the rice. When it is just about finished, toss in the diced onion so that it cooks too.

Prepare a baking dish by greasing or spraying with nonstick cooking spray.

Dump the rice into the prepared baking dish. Layer the chicken strips on top. Spread the undiluted cream of mushroom soup over the chicken.

In a small bowl, whisk together the chicken gravy with 1 cup of water, making sure to get all the lumps out. Pour this over the top of the casserole.

Cover with foil and transfer to the oven. Bake for 45 minutes or until the chicken is completely cooked.

Nutrition: Calories: 323 Fat: 56 g Carbs: 32.5 g Protein: 58.7 g Sodium: 574 mg

Campfire Chicken

Preparation Time: 10 minutes

Cooking Time: 45 minutes

Servings: 4

Ingredients:

1 tablespoon paprika

2 teaspoons onion powder

2 teaspoons salt

1 teaspoon garlic powder

1 teaspoon dried rosemary

1 teaspoon black pepper

1 teaspoon dried oregano

1 whole chicken, quartered

2 carrots, cut into thirds

3 red skin potatoes, halved

1 ear of corn, quartered

1 tablespoon olive oil

1 tablespoon butter

5 sprigs fresh thyme

Directions:

Preheat the oven to 400°F.

In a small bowl, combine the paprika, onion powder, salt, garlic powder, rosemary, pepper and oregano.

Add the chicken quarters and 1 tablespoon of the spice mix to a large plastic freezer bag. Seal and refrigerate for at least 1 hour.

Add the corn, carrots and potatoes to a large bowl. Drizzle with the olive oil and remaining spice mix. Stir or toss to coat.

Preheat a large skillet over high heat. Add some oil, and when it is hot, add the chicken pieces and cook until golden brown.

Lay out 4 pieces of aluminum foil and add some carrots, potatoes, corn and a chicken quarter to each. Top with some butter and thyme.

Fold the foil in and make pouches by sealing the edges tightly.

Bake for 45 minutes.

Nutrition: Calories: 234 Fat: 54. 4 g Carbs: 67. 9 g Protein: 76. 5 Sodium: 652 mg

Chicken and Dumplings

Preparation Time: 30 minutes

Cooking Time: 20 minutes

Servings: 4

Ingredients: 2 cups flour

½ teaspoon baking powder 1 pinch salt

2 tablespoons butter   1 scant cup buttermilk

2 quarts chicken broth

3 cups cooked chicken

Directions:

Make the dumplings by combining the flour, baking powder and salt in a large bowl. Using a pastry cutter or two knives, cut the butter into the flour mixture. Stir in the milk a little at a time until it forms a dough ball.

Cover your countertop with enough flour that the dough will not stick when you roll it out. Roll out the dough relatively thin, then cut into squares to form dumplings.

Flour a plate and transfer the dough from the counter to the plate.

Bring the chicken broth to a boil in a large saucepan, then drop the dumplings in one by one, stirring continually. The excess flour will thicken the broth. Cook for about 20 minutes or until the dumplings are no longer doughy.

Add the chicken, stir to combine, and serve.

Nutrition: Calories: 323 Fat: 78 g Carbs: 87 g Protein: 69 g Sodium: 769 mg

Chicken Pot Pie

Preparation Time: 30 minutes

Cooking Time: 30 minutes

Servings: 6 to 8

Ingredients:

½ cup butter

1 medium onion, diced

1 (14.5-ounce) can chicken broth

1 cup half and half milk

½ cup all-purpose flour

1 carrot, diced

1 celery stalk, diced

3 medium potatoes, peeled and diced

3 cups cooked chicken, diced

½ cup frozen peas

1 teaspoon chicken seasoning

½ teaspoon salt

½ teaspoon ground pepper

1 single refrigerated pie crust

1 egg

Water

Directions:

Preheat the oven to 375°F.

In a large skillet, heat the butter over medium heat, add the leeks and sauté for 3 minutes.

Sprinkle flour over the mixture, and continue to stir constantly for 3 minutes.

Whisking constantly, blend in the chicken broth and milk. Bring the mixture to a boil. Reduce heat to medium-low.

Add the carrots, celery, potatoes, salt, pepper, and stir to combine. Cook for 10-15 minutes or until veggies are cooked through but still crisp. Add chicken and peas. Stir to combine.

Transfer chicken filling to a deep 9-inch pie dish.

Fit the pie crust sheet on top and press the edges around the dish to seal the crust. Trim the excess if needed.

In a separate bowl, whisk an egg with 1 tablespoon of water, and brush the mixture over the top of the pie. With a knife, cut a few slits to let steam escape.

Bake the pie in the oven on the middle oven rack 20 to 30 minutes until the crust becomes golden brown.

Let the pie rest for about 15 minutes before serving.

Nutrition: Calories: 125 Fat: 43 g Carbs: 76 g Protein: 65 g Sodium: 545 mg

Compilation of Famous Main Dishes II

P.F. Chang's Mongolian Beef

Preparation Time: 10 minutes

Cooking Time: 20 minutes

Servings: 2

Ingredients:

1 pound flank steak

¼ cup cornstarch

2 teaspoons

½ teaspoon ginger, finely chopped

1 tablespoon ginger, diced

½ soy sauce

½ cup water

½ cup brown sugar

1 cup vegetable oil, divided

6 green onions, cut diagonally into 2-inch pieces

Directions:

Cut steak against the grain into small pieces, about ¼ inch. Transfer steak into a bowl with cornstarch and flip until fully coated on all sides. Set aside.

In a skillet, heat 1 tablespoon of the oil on medium heat. Stir in ginger and garlic. Cook for about 1 minute or until aromatic. Mix in soy sauce, water, and brown sugar. Keep stirring until sugar is melted. Bring to a boil on medium heat. Simmer for about 2 minutes or until sauce is thick.

Heat remaining vegetable oil in a separate saucepan on medium heat until oil reaches 350ºF. Deep-fry steak in batches for 2 minutes or until brown. Transfer onto a plate lined with paper towels.

Discard the oil, then add sauce and stir in meat with sauce in saucepan for about 2 minutes on medium heat. Mix in green onions and cook for an additional 1-2 minute. Place meat and onions on a plate.

Serve hot.

Nutrition: Calories: 847 Fat: 24 g Carbs: 103 g Protein: 57 g Sodium: 4176 mg

Panda Express' Beijing Beef

Preparation Time: 30 minutes

Cooking Time: 15 minutes

Servings: 4

Ingredients:

1 egg

¼ teaspoon salt

6 tablespoons water

9 tablespoons cornstarch

1 pound flank steak

4 tablespoons sugar

3 tablespoons ketchup

2 tablespoons vinegar

¼ teaspoon chili pepper, crushed

1 cup vegetable oil

1 teaspoon garlic, finely chopped

1 red bell pepper, chopped

1 green bell pepper, chopped

1 white onion, chopped

Directions:

To make the marinade, add egg, salt, 2 tablespoons water, and 1 tablespoon cornstarch in a bowl. Mix well.

Slice steak against the grain into small strips. Transfer into a Ziploc bag and pour marinade inside. Seal tightly. Shake bag gently to make sure the meat is well-coated. Set aside for at least 15 minutes.

To make the sauce, combine sugar, ketchup, vinegar, chili pepper, remaining 4 tablespoons water, and 2 teaspoons cornstarch in a bowl. Mix well. Cover and keep refrigerated.

Heat oil in a saucepan. Ready a bowl with 6 tablespoons cornstarch. Place beef in bowl and toss until fully coated. Shake off excess cornstarch and cook beef in hot oil until golden brown. Transfer onto a plate lined with paper towels.

Remove excess oil from saucepan. Toss in garlic, bell peppers, and onions and cook for about 2 minutes, stirring continuously. Transfer vegetables onto a plate.

In the same saucepan, add sauce and bring to a boil. Reduce heat to low and let simmer for 10 minutes.

Serve beef and vegetables with sauce poured on top.

Nutrition: Calories: 352 Fat: 11 g Carbs: 36 g Protein: 27 g Sodium: 355 mg

Chili from Steak n' Shake

Preparation Time: 20 minutes

Cooking Time: 6 minutes

Servings: 6

Ingredients:

1 tablespoon olive oil

2 pounds ground beef

½ teaspoon salt

2 tablespoons onion powder

1 tablespoon chili powder

2 teaspoons ground cumin

½ teaspoon ground black pepper

2 teaspoons cocoa powder

6 ounces canned tomato paste

13½ ounces canned tomato sauce

1 cup Pepsi

27 ounces canned kidney beans, rinsed and drained

Shredded cheese, sliced green onions for toppings, if desired

Directions:

Heat oil in a pan. Add beef and cook until brown, drain, then remove from heat.

In a bowl, add cooked meat, salt, onion powder, chili powder, cumin, pepper, cocoa powder, tomato paste, tomato sauce, and Pepsi. Mix until combined.

Pour mixture into a blender and puree until well blended.

Add mixture into slow cooker. Pour in beans. Cover and set slow cooker to low setting and cook for 6 hours.

Serve with shredded cheese and green onions, if desired, on top.

Nutrition: Calories: 653 Fat: 41 g Saturated fat: 17 g Carbs: 38 g Sugar: 12 g Fibers: 11 g Protein: 35 g Sodium: 1308 mg

Cracker Barrel's Meatloaf

Preparation Time: 10 minutes

Cooking Time: 1 hour and 10 minutes

Servings: 4

Ingredients:

1 pound ground beef

1 onion, chopped

1 green pepper, chopped

1 can chopped tomatoes

1 egg

½ cup frozen biscuits, shredded

1 teaspoon salt

¼ cup ketchup (optional)

Non-stick cooking spray

Directions:

Preheat oven to 350°F.

In a bowl, add beef, onion, green pepper, tomatoes, egg, biscuits, and salt. Mix well.

Using a non-stick cooking spray, coat bread pan. Then, pour meatloaf mixture into pan. Make sure the mixture is even and flat in the pan.

Place in oven and bake for about 1 hour and 5 minutes or until cooked through. Remove from oven and allow to cool for about 10 minutes.

Drain excess juice, then invert cooked meatloaf onto a serving plate. Drizzle ketchup on top, if desired. Serve.

Nutrition: Calories: 485 Fat: 32 g Saturated fat: 13 g Carbs: 27 g Sugar: 3 g Fibers: 1 g Protein: 23 g Sodium: 1273 mg

DIY Sizzling Steak, Cheese, and Mushrooms Skillet from Applebee's

Preparation Time: 15 minutes

Cooking Time: 1 hour and 35 minutes

Servings: 4

Ingredients:

1 head garlic, cut crosswise

2 tablespoons olive oil, divided

Salt and pepper, to taste

2 pounds Yukon Gold potatoes, chopped into 1-inch pieces

Water, for boiling

2 tablespoons butter

1 large yellow onion

8 ounces cremini mushrooms

Salt and pepper to taste

½ cup milk

¼ cup cream

3 tablespoons butter

2½ pounds 1-inch thick sirloin steak, cut into 4 large pieces

8 slices mozzarella cheese

Directions:

Preheat oven to 300°F.

Position garlic on foil. Pour 1 tablespoon olive oil to the inner sides where the garlic was cut, then wrap foil around garlic.

Place in oven and bake for 30 minutes. Remove from oven, and squeeze out garlic from head. Transfer to a bowl or mortar. Add salt and pepper, then mash together. Set aside.

In a pot, add potatoes. Pour enough water on top to cover potatoes. Bring to a boil. Once boiling, reduce heat to medium. Simmer for about 20 to 25 minutes or until potatoes become tender.

Melt butter on a non-stick pan over medium-low heat. Add onions and sauté for about 15 minutes until a bit tender. Toss in mushrooms and sauté, adjusting heat to medium. Season with salt and pepper. Cook for 10 minutes more. Set aside and keep warm.

Drain potatoes, then mash using an electric mixer on low speed. While mashing, gradually pour in milk, cream, butter, and mashed garlic with olive oil. Keep blending until everything is cream-like and smooth. Remove from mixer and place a cover on top of bowl. Set aside and keep warm.

Evenly coat steak pieces with remaining 1 tablespoon olive oil on all sides. Heat grill, then place meat on grill. Cook for 4 minutes. Flip and add mozzarella slices on top. Cook for another 4 minutes for medium rare. Add additional minutes for increased doneness.

Transfer steaks to serving plates then top with onion/mushroom mixture. Place mashed potatoes on the side. Serve.

Nutrition: Calories: 1159 Fat: 60 g Saturated fat: 29 g Carbs: 47 g Sugar: 4 g Fibers: 6 g Protein: 107 g Sodium: 1495 mg

Panda Express' Copycat Beef and Broccoli

Preparation Time: 30 minutes

Cooking Time: 15 minutes

Servings: 4

Ingredients: 2 tablespoons cornstarch, divided

3 tablespoons Chinese rice wine, divided

1 pound flank steak, cut thinly against the grain

1 pound broccoli florets, chopped into small pieces

2 tablespoons oyster sauce   2 tablespoons water

1 tablespoon brown sugar   1 tablespoon soy sauce

1 tablespoon cornstarch

2 tablespoons canola oil

¼ teaspoon sesame oil

1 teaspoon ginger, finely chopped

2 cloves garlic, finely chopped

2 teaspoons sesame seeds

Directions:

In a large Ziploc bag, add 1 tablespoon cornstarch and 2 tablespoons Chinese rice wine. Place beef inside and seal tightly. Massage bag to fully coat beef. Set aside to marinate for at least 20 minutes.

Rinse broccoli and place in a nonreactive bowl. Place a wet paper towel on top, then microwave for 2 minutes. Set aside.

Stir oyster sauce, water, 1 tablespoon Chinese rice wine, brown sugar, soy sauce, and remaining cornstarch in a bowl until well mixed. Set aside.

Heat wok over high heat. You want the wok to be very hot. Then, heat canola and sesame oil in wok and wait to become hot.

Working in batches, add steak and cook over high heat for 1 minute. Flip, and cook other side for another 1 minute. Transfer to a plate.

To the same wok, add garlic and ginger. Sauté for about 10 to 15 seconds then return beef to wok. Toss in heated broccoli. Slightly stir prepared sauce to make sure cornstarch is not settled on the bottom, then add to wok. Toss everything in sauce to combine. Continue cooking until sauce becomes thick. Garnish with sesame seeds. Serve.

Nutrition: Calories: 324 Fat: 17 g Saturated fat: 4g Carbs: 13 g Sugar: 6g Fibers: 3 g Protein: 28 g Sodium: 464 mg

Jack Daniel's Ribs from TGI Fridays

Preparation Time: 15 minutes

Cooking Time: 5 minutes

Servings: 4

Ingredients: 1 head garlic

1 tablespoon olive oil 1½ teaspoons paprika

½ teaspoon salt ¼ teaspoon dried thyme

½ teaspoon ground black pepper

½ teaspoon garlic powder

½ teaspoon onion powder

¼ teaspoon celery salt

¼ teaspoon ground cayenne pepper

2 racks baby back ribs

½ cup water

1 cup pineapple juice

¼ cup teriyaki sauce

1 tablespoon soy sauce

1⅓ cups dark brown sugar

3 tablespoons lemon juice

¼ cup white onion, finely chopped

2 tablespoons Jack Daniel's whiskey

1 heaping tablespoon pineapple, crushed

¼ teaspoon cayenne pepper

Directions:

Preheat oven to 300°F.

Take garlic and chop off about ½ inches from the head. Take out paper-like outer layers then place in a small oven-safe bowl or ramekin. Pour olive oil on top and wrap in aluminum foil. Place in oven and bake for 1 hour. When ready, remove from oven and allow to cool. Squeeze out about garlic from roasted garlic head. Add roasted garlic in an airtight container and place in refrigerator

While the garlic is baking, prepare the spice rub by combining paprika, salt, thyme, pepper, garlic powder, onion powder, celery salt, and ground cayenne pepper in a bowl. Mix well. Evenly coat ribs with spice rub. Arrange ribs onto a baking sheet. Bake in oven for about 2½ hours.

Prepare the barbecue sauce by mixing water, pineapple juice, teriyaki sauce, soy sauce, and dark brown sugar in a pan. Bring to a boil while stirring from time to time. Once boiling, lower heat until mixture is just simmering.

Add to pan 2 teaspoons of the roasted garlic, lemon juice, onion, whiskey, crushed pineapple, and cayenne pepper. Stir to combine well. Simmer for about 30 to 40 minutes until liquid is reduced by half.

If desired, you can finish the ribs on the barbecue to have grilling marks and crisper ribs. Preheat grill to medium-high heat. Then, place ribs onto grill and cook for about 2 to 4 minutes. Turn ribs over and grill for another 2 to 4 minutes.

Transfer onto a serving plate. Spoon sauce over ribs. Serve.

Nutrition: Calories: 779 Fat: 38 g Saturated fat: 13 g Carbs: 80 g

Sugar: 77 g Fibers: 1 g Protein: 29 g Sodium: 865 mg

Smokehouse Pork Belly Sandwich from Arby's

Preparation Time: 15 minutes

Cooking Time: 2 hours and 30 minutes

Servings: 6

Ingredients:

2 pounds center cut pork belly

Salt and pepper, to taste

1-2 tablespoons barbecue spice rub

6 star cross buns

Cooking spray

½ pound smoked cheddar cheese

½ cup mayonnaise

½ cup any smoky barbecue sauce

6 ounces onion strings

Directions:

Sprinkle salt and pepper onto pork belly then coat with barbecue rub.

Set smoker to 300°F with hickory wood on coals. Put pork belly in smoker with fat side facing down.

Smoke for about 2½ hours until well browned and a bit charred. Pork is ready once its internal temperature is about 185 to 195°F.

Spray cooking spray onto the inner sides of buns then toast until golden brown.

Assemble sandwich by layering mayo, cooked pork belly, barbecue sauce, cheese, and onion strings on the bottom bun. Top with second bun. Repeat for remaining sandwiches.

Serve.

Nutrition: Calories: 1351 Fat: 117 g Saturated fat: 41 g Carbs: 45 g Sugar: 13 g Fibers: 2 g Protein: 29 g Sodium: 1023 mg

Red Beans and Rice from Popeye's

Preparation Time: 20 minutes

Cooking Time: 40 minutes

Servings: 10

Ingredients:

3 14-ounce cans red beans

¾ pounds smoked ham hock

1¼ cups water

½ teaspoon onion powder

½ teaspoon garlic salt

¼ teaspoon red pepper flakes

½ teaspoon salt

3 tablespoons lard

Steamed long-grain rice

Directions:

Add 2 canned red beans, ham hock, and water to pot. Cook on medium heat and let simmer for about 1 hour.

Remove from heat and wait until meat is cool enough to handle. Then, remove meat from bone.

In a food processor, add meat, cooked red beans and water mixture, onion powder, garlic salt, red pepper, salt, and lard. Pulse for 4 seconds. You want the beans to be cut and the liquid thickened. Drain remaining 1 can red beans and add to food processor. Pulse for only 1 or 2 seconds.

Remove ingredients from food processor and transfer to the pot from earlier. Cook on low heat, stirring frequently until mixture is heated through.

Serve over steamed rice.

Nutrition: Calories: 445 Fat: 12 g Saturated fat: 4g Carbs: 67 g Sugar: 1 g Fibers: 9 g Protein: 17 g Sodium: 670 mg

Café Rio's Sweet Pork Barbacoa Salad

Preparation Time: 10 minutes

Cooking Time: 8 minutes

Servings: 8

Ingredients:

3 pounds pork loin

Garlic salt, to taste

1 can root beer

¼ cup water

¾ cup brown sugar

1 10-ounce can red enchilada sauce

1 4-ounce can green chilies

½ teaspoon chili powder

8 large burrito size tortillas

1½ serving Cilantro Lime Rice

1 can black beans, drained and heated

2 heads Romaine lettuce, shredded

1½ cups tortilla strips

1 cup Queso Fresco cheese

2 limes, cut in wedges

¼ cup cilantro

Dressing:

½ packet Hidden Valley Ranch Dressing Mix

1 cup mayonnaise

½ cup milk

½ cup cilantro leaves

¼ cup salsa verde

½ jalapeno pepper, deseeded

1 plump clove garlic

2 tablespoons fresh lime juice

Directions:

Sprinkle garlic salt on pork. Put in slow cooker with the fat side facing down. Add ¼ cup root beer and water. Cover and cook on low setting for 6 hours.

To prepare sauce add the rest of the root beer, brown sugar, enchilada sauce, green chilies, and chili powder in a blender. Blend until smooth.

Remove meat from slow cooker then transfer onto cutting board. Shred, discarding juices and fat. Return shredded pork to slow cooker with sauce. Cook on low setting for another 2 hours. When there is only about 15 to 20 minutes left to cook, remove lid to thicken sauce.

To prepare dressing mix all dressing ingredients in a blender. Puree until smooth. Then, transfer to refrigerator and allow to chill for at least 1 hour.

To assemble salad, layer tortilla, rice, beans, pork, lettuce, tortilla strips, cheese, and dressing in a bowl. Serve with a lime wedge and cilantro leaves.

Nutrition: Calories: 756 Fat: 28 g Saturated fat: 7 g Carbs: 91 g Sugar: 31 g Fibers: 7 g Protein: 38 g Sodium: 1389 mg

Edo Japan's Sukiyaki Beef

Preparation Time: 15 minutes

Cooking Time: 5 to 6 minutes

Marinating Time: 20 minutes

Servings: 2 to 4

Ingredients:

10 ounces sirloin steak, thinly sliced

½ carrot, thinly sliced

½ onion, sliced

1 green pepper, sliced

½ yellow bell pepper, sliced

½ cup sukiyaki sauce, divided

1 tablespoon oil

1 teaspoon chopped garlic

2 tablespoons ginger, finely chopped

2 teaspoons soy sauce

1 teaspoon sugar

1 tablespoon oyster sauce

Directions:

Pour half of the sukiyaki sauce into a medium bowl and add the sliced beef. Let the beef marinate for 20 minutes.

Heat the oil in a large skillet. Add the garlic and cook for about 30 seconds.

Add the beef, with the sauce. Cook over medium-high heat until the beef is cooked through.

Add the ginger, carrots, peppers and onions and cook until the veggies have begun to soften.

Add the rest of the sukiyaki sauce along with the oyster sauce, soy sauce and sugar. Cook and stir for about 2 more minutes.

Serve over rice.

Nutrition: Calories: 152 Fat:24 g Carbs: 20 g Protein: 5.6 g Sodium: 627 mg

Compilation of Main Dishes III

Chicken Fried Chicken

Preparation Time: 15 minutes

Cooking Time: 30 minutes

Servings: 4

Ingredients:

Chicken

½ cup all-purpose flour

1 teaspoon poultry seasoning

½ teaspoon salt

½ teaspoon pepper

1 egg, slightly beaten

1 tablespoon water

4 boneless skinless chicken breasts, pounded to ½-inch thickness

1 cup vegetable oil

Gravy

2 tablespoons all-purpose flour

¼ teaspoon salt

¼ teaspoon pepper

1¼ cups milk

Directions:

Preheat the oven to 200°F.

In a shallow dish, combine the flour, poultry seasoning, salt and pepper.

In another shallow dish, mix together the beaten egg and water.

First dip both sides of the chicken breasts in the flour mixture, then dip them in the egg mixture, and then back into the flour mixture.

Heat the vegetable oil over medium-high heat in a large deep skillet. A cast iron is good choice if you have one. Add the chicken and cook for about 15 minutes, or until fully cooked, turning over about halfway through.

Transfer the chicken to a cookie sheet and place in the oven to maintain temperature.

Remove all but 2 tablespoons of oil from the skillet you cooked the chicken in.

Prepare the gravy by whisking the dry gravy ingredients together in a bowl. Then whisk them into the oil in the skillet, stirring thoroughly to remove lumps. When the flour begins to brown, slowly whisk in the milk. Continue cooking and whisking for about 2 minutes or until the mixture thickens.

Top chicken with some of the gravy.

Nutrition: Calories: 234 Fat: 24 g Carbs: 54 g Protein: 61 g Sodium: 1286 mg

Broccoli Cheddar Chicken

Preparation Time: 10 minutes

Cooking Time: 45 minutes

Servings: 4

Ingredients:

4 skinless chicken breasts

1 cup milk

1 cup Ritz-style crackers, crushed

1 (10.5-ounce) can condensed cheddar cheese soup

½ pound frozen broccoli

6 ounces cheddar cheese, shredded

½ teaspoon salt

½ teaspoon pepper

Directions:

Preheat the oven to 350°F.

Whisk the milk and cheddar cheese soup together in a mixing bowl.

Prepare a baking dish by greasing the sides, then lay the chicken in the bottom and season with the salt and pepper.

Pour the soup mixture over the chicken, then top with the crackers, broccoli and shredded cheese.

Bake for about 45 minutes or until bubbly.

Nutrition: Calories: 343 Fat: 43 g Carbs: 54 g Protein: 16 g Sodium: 565 mg

Cajun Jambalaya Pasta

Preparation Time: 10 minutes

Cooking Time: 50 minutes

Servings: 6

Ingredients:

¼ cup unsalted butter

¼ cup extra-virgin olive oil

1 pound andouille sausage or smoked sausage, sliced

1 pound boneless skinless chicken breast, cubed

1 bell pepper, diced

1 white onion, diced

3 stalks celery, diced

4 cloves garlic, minced

1 pound jumbo shrimp, peeled and deveined

2 cups red salsa

1 (6 -ounce) can hot tomato sauce

1 quart low-sodium chicken broth

1 bay leaf

¼ cup Italian parsley, chopped

½ bunch green onions

1 pound linguine pasta, cooked according to the package directions

Spice Blend

1 tablespoon creole seasoning

1 tablespoon garlic powder

1 tablespoon onion powder

2 teaspoons black pepper

1 teaspoon paprika

Pinch cayenne pepper

Garlic bread, for serving

Directions:

In a small dish, mix together all the spices for the spice blend.

Season the chicken chunks with 1 tablespoon of the spice blend. Mix until the chicken is well coated, and set it aside.

In a large saucepan, melt the butter and heat olive oil over medium heat.

When it is hot, add the sausage slices and cook for 5 minutes. Add the chicken and cook for about 10 minutes.

Next, add the bell pepper, onion, and celery. Mix in half of the remaining spice blend. Cook for approximately 10 minutes, then add the garlic and cook 1 more minute.

With 1 tablespoon of seasoning blend, season the shrimp and set it aside. Then add the rest of the spices to the saucepan and stir to combine.

Add the salsa, tomato sauce, chicken broth, and the bay leaf. Mix together and bring it to a boil, stirring it together so that everything is well combined. Don't forget to scrape the bottom of the pan for brown bits.

Reduce the heat and let it simmer, covered, for about 30 minutes. Once the 30 minutes is up, discard the bay leaf. Add the shrimp, parsley, and green onions, and cook, still covered for about 10 minutes more.

Serve over pasta with a slice of toasted garlic bread.

Nutrition: Calories: 234 Fat: 53 g Carbs: 65 g Protein: 62 g Sodium: 652 mg

Grilled Chicken Tenderloin

Preparation Time: 10 minutes

Marinating Time: 1 hour

Cooking Time: 30 min

Servings: 4 to 5

Ingredients:

4-5 boneless and skinless chicken breasts, cut into strips, or 12 chicken tenderloins, tendons removed

1 cup Italian dressing

2 teaspoons lime juice

4 teaspoons honey

Directions:

Combine the dressing, lime juice and honey in a plastic bag. Seal and shake to combine.

Place the chicken in the bag. Seal and shake again, then transfer to the refrigerator for at least 1 hour. The longer it marinates, the more the flavors will infuse into the chicken.

When ready to prepare, transfer the chicken and the marinade to a large nonstick skillet.

Bring to a boil, then reduce the heat and allow simmering until the liquid has cooked down to a glaze.

Nutrition: Calories: 451 Fat: 43 g Carbs: 61 g Protein: 65.7 g Sodium: 526 mg

Miso Glazed Salmon

Preparation Time: 10 minutes

Cooking Time: 10 minutes

Servings: 4

Ingredients:

½ cup brown sugar

3 tablespoons soy sauce

¼ cup hot water

3 tablespoons miso (soybean paste)

4 salmon fillets

1 tablespoon butter

2 tablespoons ginger paste

1 tablespoon garlic paste

½ cup sake

1 tablespoon heavy cream

½ cup butter, cut into 8 pieces

Juice of half of a lime

For serving:

Steamed snow peas, broccoli, and carrots

Steamed Jasmine Rice

Directions:

Preheat the broiler.

Mix together the brown sugar, soy sauce, hot water, and miso paste. Stir until well combined.

Lightly oil a baking dish and arrange the salmon fillets in it. Spoon some of the miso mixture over each fillet, leaving some for basting. Transfer the pan to the oven and broil for about 10 minutes. Baste every 3 minutes while broiling.

In the meantime, in a small saucepan, melt 1 tablespoon of butter over medium-high heat. Add the ginger and garlic paste, and cook for about 2 minutes.

Stir in the sake and bring the mixture to a boil. Let it cook for 3 more minutes, and add the heavy cream. Cook another 2 minutes, or until the sauce starts to reduce. Then whisk in the remaining butter one piece at a time and cook until the sauce thickens. Remove the saucepan from the heat and stir in the lime juice.

When the salmon is done, serve by pouring a little sauce over the rice and top with a salmon fillet with vegetables on the side.

Nutrition: Calories: 234 Fat: 34.9 g Carbs: 43 g Protein: 45 g Sodium: 524 mg

Almond Crusted Salmon Salad

Preparation Time: 15 minutes

Cooking Time: 30 minutes

Servings: 4

Ingredients:

¼ cup olive oil

4 (4 -ounce) portions salmon

½ teaspoon kosher salt

⅛ teaspoon ground black pepper

2 tablespoons garlic aioli (bottled is fine)

½ cup chopped and ground almonds for crust

10 ounces kale, chopped

¼ cup lemon dressing of choice

2 avocados, peeled, pitted and cut into ½-inch pieces

2 cups cooked quinoa

1 cup brussels sprouts, sliced

2 ounces arugula

½ cup dried cranberries

1 cup balsamic vinaigrette

24 thin radish slices

Lemon zest

Directions:

In a large skillet, heat the olive oil over medium-high heat. Sprinkle the salmon with salt and pepper to season. When the skillet is hot, add the fish fillets and cook for about 3 minutes on each side, or until it flakes easily with a fork. Top the salmon with garlic aioli and sprinkle with nuts.

Meanwhile, combine all the salad ingredients, including the quinoa, in a bowl and toss with the dressing.

Serve the salad with a fish fillet on top of greens and sprinkle with radishes and lemon zest.

Nutrition: Calories: 243 Fat: 45 g Carbs: 23 g Protein: 52 g Sodium: 1436 mg

Shrimp Scampi

Preparation Time: 10 minutes

Cooking Time: 30 minutes

Servings: 4

Ingredients:

1-2 pounds fresh shrimp, cleaned, deveined, and butterflied

1 cup milk

3 tablespoons olive oil

½ cup all-purpose flour

4 tablespoons Parmesan cheese, divided

¼ teaspoon salt

½ teaspoon fresh ground black pepper

¼ teaspoon cayenne pepper

6-8 whole garlic cloves

1 cup dry white wine

2 cups heavy cream

5-7 leaves fresh basil, cut into strips

1 diced tomato

2 tablespoons Parmesan cheese, finely grated

1 shallot, diced

1 pound angel hair pasta, cooked (hot)

Parsley, to garnish

Directions:

Put the shrimp in the milk and let it sit.

In a shallow bowl, combine the flour, 2 tablespoons of Parmesan, salt, pepper, and cayenne.

Pour the olive oil in a large skillet, making sure it's enough to cover the bottom. Heat over medium-high heat.

Take the shrimp from the milk and dredge in flour mixture. Transfer it to the skillet and cook about 2 minutes on each side. After the shrimp cooks, transfer it to a plate covered with a paper towel to drain.

Reduce the heat to medium-low and cook the garlic in the leftover oil. (Don't worry about any bits left from the shrimp because these will add flavor and help to thicken the sauce.)

After the garlic cooks for a couple of minutes, add the wine. Increase the heat and bring the mixture to a boil, then reduce the heat and simmer to reduce liquid to about half of the original volume.

Add the cream and simmer for about 10 more minutes, then add the basil, tomato, cheese, and shallots. Stir to combine.

Add the shrimp to the skillet and remove it from the heat.

Arrange the pasta on serving plates, topped with shrimp and covered with sauce. Garnish with parsley.

Nutrition: Calories: 454 Fat: 54 g Carbs: 152 g Protein: 41 g Sodium: 1614 mg

Copycat Wendy's Beef Chili

Preparation Time: 15 minutes

Cooking Time: 1 hour and 20 minutes

Servings: 10

Ingredients:

2 tablespoons olive oil

2 pounds ground beef

2 stalks celery, diced

1 onion, diced

1 green bell pepper, diced

3 14-ounce cans stewed tomatoes

1 10-ounce can diced tomatoes with green chiles (such as Ro*Tel)

1 14-ounce can tomato sauce

1 cup water

2 1¼- ounce packages chili seasoning

1 14-ounce can kidney beans, not drained

1 14-ounce can pinto beans, not drained

Salt and ground black pepper to taste

1 tablespoon white vinegar

Directions:

In a pot, cook oil on medium-high heat. Add beef and cook for 8-10 minutes or until beef is brown, crumbly, and cooked through.

Toss in celery, onion, and bell pepper into pot. Sauté for 5 minutes or until fragrant. Add stewed and diced tomatoes, green chilies, tomato sauce, and water. Stir until there are no more big chunks from the stewed tomatoes, then mix in chili seasoning.

Add kidney and pinto beans into pot. Sprinkle salt and pepper, to taste. Stir, and bring to a boil. Then reduce heat to a simmer. Simmer for about 1 hour on low heat. Stir in vinegar. Serve hot.

Nutrition: Calories: 326 Fat: 15 g Carbs: 29 g Protein: 23 g Sodium: 1521 mg

The Mexican Pizza from Taco Bell

Preparation Time: 30 minutes

Cooking Time: 12 minutes

Servings: 4

Ingredients:

½ pound ground beef

½ teaspoon salt

¼ teaspoon onion, finely chopped

¼ teaspoon paprika

1½ teaspoon chili powder

2 tablespoons water

1 cup vegetable oil

8 6-inch flour tortillas

1 16-ounce can refried beans

⅔ cup picante sauce

⅓ cup tomato, finely chopped

1 cup cheddar cheese, grated

1 cup Colby jack cheese, grated

¼ cup green onion, diced

¼ cup black olives, chopped

Directions:

Preheat oven to 400°F.

In a skillet, sauté beef on medium heat. Once brown, drain. Then stir in salt, onions, paprika, chili powder, and water. While continuously stirring, cook for an additional 10 minutes.

In a separate skillet add oil and heat over medium-high. Cook tortilla for about 30 seconds on both sides or until golden brown. Use a fork to pierce any bubbles forming on the tortillas. Transfer onto a plate lined with paper towels.

Microwave refried beans on high for about 30 seconds or until warm.

To build each pizza, coat ⅓ cup beans on tortilla followed by ⅓ cup cooked beef. Top with a second tortilla. Cover with 2 tablespoons picante sauce, then equal amounts of tomatoes, cheeses, green onions, and olives. This makes a total of 4 pizzas.

Place prepared pizzas on baking sheet. Bake in oven until cheese is fully melted, about 8 to 12 minutes.

Serve.

Nutrition: Calories: 1218 Fat: 90 g Carbs: 66 g Protein: 39 g Sodium: 2038 mg

Copycat Swedish Meatballs from Ikea

Preparation Time: 30 minutes

Cooking Time: 30 minutes

Servings: 2

Ingredients:

3 tablespoons butter, divided

1¼ tablespoon onion, minced

1 boiled potato, cold

¼ ground beef

¼ ground pork

1 egg

¼ cup milk

¼ cup water

⅛ cup breadcrumbs

Salt, to taste

White pepper, to taste

Sauce

1 tablespoon all-purpose flour

1 tablespoon butter

½ cup beef stock

¼ cup cream

For serving

Boiled potatoes

Lingonberry jam

Directions:

To make the meatballs, melt 2 tablespoons of the butter in a pan over medium-high heat. Add onion and cook until transparent, about 1-2 minutes.

In a bowl, mash a potato. Then, combine with cooked onion, beef, pork, egg, milk, water, and breadcrumbs. Season salt and white pepper, to taste.

Flour cutting board and form meat into round 1-inch balls.

In previous pan, melt remaining butter and cook on low heat until meatballs are cooked through, about 4-6 minutes, stirring a few times. Don't overcrowd the pan, work in batch if needed.

Transfer to a plate and cover with foil to keep warm.

To make the sauce, heat butter in a saucepan over medium heat. Stir in flour and cook until golden brown. Pour in stock and cream, and whisk until smooth. Flavor with salt and pepper, to taste.

Pour sauce onto meatballs and serve with boiled potatoes and lingonberry jam.

Nutrition: Calories: 1172 Fat: 87 g Carbs: 45 g Protein: 52 g Sodium: 520 mg

Desserts

Cinnamon Apple Turnover

Preparation Time: 10 minutes

Cooking Time: 25 minutes

Servings: 4 to 6

Ingredients:

1 large Granny Smith apple, peeled, cored, and diced

½ teaspoon cornstarch

¼ teaspoon cinnamon

Dash ground nutmeg

¼ cup brown sugar

¼ cup applesauce

¼ teaspoon vanilla extract

1 tablespoon butter, melted

1 sheet of puff pastry, thawed

Whipped cream or vanilla ice cream, to serve

Directions:

Preheat the oven to 400°F.

Prepare a baking sheet by spraying it with non-stick cooking spray or using a bit of oil on a paper towel.

In a mixing bowl, mix together the apples, cornstarch, cinnamon, nutmeg, and brown sugar. Stir to make sure the apples are well covered with the spices. Then stir in the applesauce and the vanilla.

Lay out your puff pastry and cut it into squares. You should be able to make 4 or 6 depending on how big you want your turnovers to be and how big your pastry is.

Place some of the apple mixture in the center of each square and fold the corners of the pastry up to make a pocket. Pinch the edges together to seal. Then brush a bit of the melted butter over the top to give the turnovers that nice brown color.

Place the filled pastry onto the prepared baking pan and transfer to the preheated oven. Bake 20–25 minutes, or until they become a golden brown in color.

Serve with whipped cream or vanilla ice cream.

Nutrition: Calories: 332 Fat: 24 g Carbs: 65 g Protein: 76 g Sodium: 767 mg

Cherry Chocolate Cobbler

Preparation Time: 10 minutes

Cooking Time: 45 minutes

Servings: 8

Ingredients:

1½ cups all-purpose flour

½ cup sugar

2 teaspoons baking powder

½ teaspoon salt

¼ cup butter

6 ounces semisweet chocolate morsels

¼ cup milk

1 egg, beaten

21 ounces cherry pie filling

½ cup finely chopped nuts

Directions:

Preheat the oven to 350°F.

Combine the flour, sugar, baking powder, salt and butter in a large mixing bowl. Use a pastry blender to cut the mixture until there are lumps the size of small peas.

Melt the chocolate morsels. Let cool for approximately 5 minutes, then add the milk and egg and mix well. Beat into the flour mixture, mixing completely.

Spread the pie filling in a 2-quart casserole dish. Randomly drop the chocolate batter over the filling, and then sprinkle with nuts.

Bake for 40–45 minutes.

Serve with a scoop of vanilla ice cream if desired.

Nutrition: Calories: 243 Fat: 41 g Carbs: 75 g Protein: 67 g Sodium: 879 mg

Chocolate Pecan Pie

Preparation Time: 10 minutes

Cooking Time: 50 minutes

Servings: 8

Ingredients:

3 eggs

½ cup sugar

1 cup corn syrup

½ teaspoon salt

1 teaspoon vanilla extract

¼ cup melted butter

1 cup pecans

3 tablespoons semisweet chocolate chips

1 unbaked pie shell

Directions:

Preheat the oven to 350°F.

Beat together the eggs and sugar in a mixing bowl, then add the corn syrup, salt, vanilla and butter.

Put the chocolate chips and pecans inside the pie shell and pour the egg mixture over the top.

Bake for 50-60 minutes or until set.

Serve with vanilla ice cream.

Nutrition: Calories: 465 Fat: 76 g Carbs: 37 g Protein: 97 g Sodium: 4461 mg

Pumpkin Custard with Gingersnaps

Preparation Time: 30 minutes

Cooking Time: 35 minutes

Servings: 8

Ingredients:

Custard

8 egg yolks

1¾ cups (1 15-ounce can) pure pumpkin puree

1¾ cups heavy whipping cream

½ cup sugar

1½ teaspoons pumpkin pie spice

1 teaspoon vanilla

Topping

1 cup crushed gingersnap cookies

1 tablespoon melted butter

Whipped Cream

1 cup heavy whipping cream

1 tablespoon superfine sugar (or regular sugar if you have no caster sugar)

½ teaspoon pumpkin pie spice

Garnish

8 whole gingersnap cookies

Directions:

Preheat the oven to 350°F.

Separate the yolks from 8 eggs and whisk them together in a large mixing bowl until they are well blended and creamy.

Add the pumpkin, sugar, vanilla, heavy cream and pumpkin pie spice and whisk to combine.

Cook the custard mixture in a double boiler, stirring until it has thickened enough that it coats a spoon.

Pour the mixture into individual custard cups or an 8×8-inch baking pan and bake for about 20 minutes if using individual cups or 30–35 minutes for the baking pan, until it is set, and a knife inserted comes out clean.

While the custard is baking, make the topping by combining the crushed gingersnaps and melted butter. After the custard has been in the oven for 15 minutes, sprinkle the gingersnap mixture over the top.

When the custard has passed the clean knife test, remove from the oven and let cool to room temperature.

Whisk the heavy cream and pumpkin pie spice together with the caster sugar and beat just until it thickens.

Serve the custard with the whipped cream and garnish each serving with a gingersnap.

Nutrition: Calories: 255 Fat: 35 g Carbs: 25 g Protein: 76 g Sodium: 877 mg

Baked Apple Dumplings

Preparation Time: 20 minutes

Cooking Time: 40 minutes

Servings: 2 to 4

Ingredients:

1 (17½ ounce) package frozen puff pastry, thawed

1 cup sugar

6 tablespoons dry breadcrumbs

2 teaspoons ground cinnamon

1 pinch ground nutmeg

1 egg, beaten

4 Granny Smith apples, peeled, cored and halved

Vanilla ice cream for serving

Icing

1 cup confectioners' sugar

1 teaspoon vanilla extract

3 tablespoons milk

Pecan Streusel

⅔ cup chopped toasted pecans

⅔ cup packed brown sugar

⅔ cup all-purpose flour

5 tablespoons melted butter

Directions:

Preheat the oven to 425°F.

When the puff pastry has completely thawed, roll out each sheet to measure 12 inches by 12 inches. Cut the sheets into quarters.

Combine the sugar, breadcrumbs, cinnamon and nutmeg together in a small bowl.

Brush one of the pastry squares with some of the beaten egg. Add about 1 tablespoon of the breadcrumb mixture on top, then add half an apple, core side down, over the crumbs. Add another tablespoon of the breadcrumb mixture.

Seal the dumpling by pulling up the corners and pinching the pastry together until the seams are totally sealed. Repeat this process with the remaining squares.

Assemble the ingredients for the pecan streusel in a small bowl.

Grease a baking sheet, or line it with parchment paper. Place the dumplings on the sheet and brush them with a bit more of the beaten egg. Top with the pecan streusel.

Bake for 15 minutes, then reduce heat to 350°F and bake for 25 minutes more or until lightly browned.

Make the icing by combining the confectioners' sugar, vanilla and milk until you reach the proper consistency.

When the dumplings are done, let them cool to room temperature and drizzle them with icing before serving.

Nutrition: Calories:145 Fat: 57 g Carbs: 87 g Protein: 66.9 g Sodium: 529 mg

Peach Cobbler

Preparation Time: 10 minutes

Cooking Time: 45 minutes

Servings: 4

Ingredients:

1¼ cups Bisquick

1 cup milk

½ cup melted butter

¼ teaspoon nutmeg

½ teaspoon cinnamon

Vanilla ice cream, for serving

Filling

1 (30-ounce) can peaches in syrup, drained

¼ cup sugar

Topping

½ cup brown sugar

¼ cup almond slices

½ teaspoon cinnamon

1 tablespoon melted butter

Directions:

Preheat the oven to 375°F.

Grease the bottom and sides of an 8×8-inch pan.

Whisk together the Bisquick, milk, butter, nutmeg and cinnamon in a large mixing bowl. When thoroughly combined, pour into the greased baking pan.

Mix together the peaches and sugar in another mixing bowl. Put the filling on top of the batter in the pan. Bake for about 45 minutes.

In another bowl, mix together the brown sugar, almonds, cinnamon, and melted butter. After the cobbler has cooked for 45 minutes, cover evenly with the topping and bake for an additional 10 minutes.

Serve with a scoop of vanilla ice cream.

Nutrition: Calories: 168 Fat: 76 g Carbs: 15 g Protein: 78.9 g Sodium: 436 mg

Royal Dansk Butter Cookies

Preparation Time: 15 minutes

Cooking Time: 25 minutes

Servings: 10

Ingredients:

120g cake flour, sifted

½ teaspoon vanilla extract

25g powdered sugar

120g softened butter, at room temperature

A pinch of sea salt, approximately ¼ teaspoon

Directions:

Using a hand mixer; beat the butter with sugar, vanilla & salt until almost doubled in mass & lightened to a yellowish-white in color, for 8 to 10 minutes, on low to middle speed.

Scrape the mixture from the sides of yours bowl using a rubber spatula. Sift the flour x 3 times & gently fold in until well incorporated.

Transfer the mixture into a sheet of plastic wrap, roll into log & cut a hole on it; placing it into the piping bag attached with a nozzle flower tips 4.6cm/1.81" x 1.18".

Pipe each cookie into 5cm wide swirls on a parchment paper lined baking tray.

Cover & place them in a freezer until firm up, for 30 minutes.

Preheat your oven to 300 F in advance. Once done; bake until the edges start to turn golden, for 20 minutes.

Let completely cool on the cooling rack before serving.

Store them in an airtight container.

Nutrition: Calories: 455 Fat: 67 g Carbs: 12. 8 g Protein: 66.3 g Sodium: 552 mg

Campfire S'mores

Preparation Time: 15 minutes

Cooking Time: 40 minutes

Servings: 9

Ingredients:

Graham Cracker Crust

2 cups graham cracker crumbs

¼ cup sugar

½ cup butter

½ teaspoon cinnamon

1 small package brownie mix (enough for an 8×8-inch pan), or use the brownie ingredients listed below.

Brownie Mix

½ cup flour

⅓ cup cocoa

¼ teaspoon baking powder

¼ teaspoon salt

½ cup butter

1 cup sugar

1 teaspoon vanilla

2 large eggs

S'mores Topping

9 large marshmallows

5 Hershey candy bars

4½ cups vanilla ice cream

½ cup chocolate sauce

Directions:

Preheat the oven to 350°F.

Mix together the graham cracker crumbs, sugar, cinnamon and melted butter in a medium bowl. Stir until the crumbs and sugar have combined with the butter.

Line an 8×8-inch baking dish with parchment paper. Make sure to use enough so that you'll be able to lift the baked brownies out of the dish easily. Press the graham cracker mixture into the bottom of the lined pan.

Place pan in the oven to prebake the crust a bit while you are making the brownie mixture.

Melt the butter over medium heat in a large saucepan, then stir in the sugar and vanilla. Whisk in the eggs one at a time. Then whisk in the dry ingredients, followed by the nuts. Mix until smooth. Take the crust out of the oven, pour the mixture into it, and bake for 23–25 minutes. When brownies are done, remove from oven and let cool in the pan.

After the brownies have cooled completely, lift them out of the pan using the edges of the parchment paper. Be careful not to crack or break the brownies. Cut into individual slices.

When you are ready to serve, place a marshmallow on top of each brownie and broil in the oven until the marshmallow starts to brown. You can also microwave for a couple of seconds, but you won't get the browning that you would in the broiler.

Remove from the oven and top each brownie with half of a Hershey bar. Serve with ice cream and a drizzle of chocolate sauce.

Nutrition: Calories: 187 Fat: 18.9 g Carbs: 56.6 g Protein: 65. 2 Sodium: 552 mg

Banana Pudding

Preparation Time: 15 minutes

Cooking Time: 1 hour and 30 minutes

Servings: 8 to 10

Ingredients:

6 cups milk

5 eggs, beaten

¼ teaspoon vanilla extract

1⅛ cups flour

1½ cups sugar

¾ pound vanilla wafers

3 bananas, peeled

8 ounces Cool Whip or 2 cups of whipped cream

Directions:

In a large saucepan, heat the milk to about 170°F.

Mix the eggs, vanilla, flour, and sugar together in a large bowl.

Very slowly add the egg mixture to the warned milk and cook until the mixture thickens to a custard consistency.

Layer the vanilla wafers to cover the bottom of a baking pan or glass baking dish. You can also use individual portion dessert dish or glasses.

Layer banana slices over the top of the vanilla wafers. Be as liberal with the bananas as you want.

Layer the custard mixture on top of the wafers and bananas. Move the pan to the refrigerator and cool for 1½ hours. When ready to serve, spread Cool Whip (or real whipped cream, if you prefer) over the top. Garnish with banana slices and wafers if desired.

Nutrition: Calories: 166 Fat: 56 g Carbs: 78.9 g Protein: 47.8 g Sodium: 578 mg

Molten Chocolate Cake

Preparation Time: 1 hour 30 minutes

Cooking Time: 30 minutes

Servings: 8 to 10

Ingredients:

1 Duncan Hines fudge cake mix

3 large eggs

1 cup milk

½ cup oil

½ cup sour cream

Vanilla ice cream

Chocolate shell ice cream topping

Caramel sauce

For Magic Shell

¼ cup coconut oil

2 cups chocolate chips, semi-sweet

For Hot Fudge

1 bag semi-sweet chocolate chips (12-ounces)

4 tablespoons unsalted butter

1 can sweetened condensed milk (14-ounces)

A pinch of salt

1 teaspoon pure vanilla extract

Directions:

Stir the dry cake mix together with sour cream, eggs, milk & oil in a large bowl.

Lightly coat a large-sized cupcake pan with the nonstick spray & distribute the batter evenly approximately ¾ full. Bake as per the directions mentioned on the package.

Turn the cakes out onto their tops creating a "volcano" & let cool.

Gently cut a hole out of the middle without going clear to the bottom using a pairing or serrated knife.

Fill with cool hot fudge & then slice off the bottom circle of the piece of cake you removed and place it on the hot fudge hole like a lid.

Using a plastic wrap; cover & let chill in a fridge for 30 minutes.

Remove the cakes from freezer & reheat in the microwave for half a minute, until warm.

Top with caramel, ice cream & magic shell.

For Magic Shell

Place the chocolate along with the coconut oil in a microwave safe bowl and slowly heat for 30 second intervals until melted, stirring often.

Serve over cold ice cream & it would harden.

For Hot Fudge

Melt the entire ingredients together over medium heat in a medium saucepan.

Bring the mixture to a boil, stirring every now and then.

Continue to boil & stir for a minute or two more.

Remove the pan from heat & continue to stir for a minute.

Let the fudge sauce to cool.

Nutrition: Calories: 146 Fat: 64.5 g Carbs: 77. 6 g Protein: 63.8 g Sodium: 766 mg

Paradise Pie

Preparation Time: 10 minutes

Cooking Time: 1 hour and 5 minutes

Servings: 6

Ingredients:

For Crust:

3 tablespoon granulated sugar

⅓ cup graham cracker crumbs

3 tablespoon butter

⅓ cup chocolate chips

For Filling:

½ cup flour

¼ cup coconut, shredded

¾ teaspoon baking powder

⅓ cup milk

¼ cup walnuts, crushed

1 teaspoon vanilla extract

¼ cup granulated sugar

⅓ cup semisweet chocolate chips

1 tablespoon canola oil

For Topping:

Vanilla ice cream

2 tablespoon butter

Hot fudge

¼ cup walnuts, chopped or crushed

Caramel topping

Directions:

For Crust:

Preheat oven to 350 F.

Now, in a medium-sized microwave-safe bowl; heat the butter until completely melted. When done, add in the graham cracker crumbs & sugar; mix well.

Transfer to a 1-quart casserole dish. Firmly pressing into the bottom of your dish. Evenly top with the chocolate chips.

Bake in the preheated oven until the chocolate is completely melted, for 5 minutes. Spread the melted chocolate out smoothly using a rubber spatula.

For Filling:

Combine the entire dry ingredients in a large-sized mixing bowl. Add oil, milk & vanilla; mix on low speed until completely smooth.

With mixer still on low, add in the coconut, chocolate chips & walnuts.

When mixed thoroughly, pour the filling on top of the crust.

Bake at 350 F until a wooden pick comes out clean, for 35 to 40 minutes, uncovered.

To Serve:

Spoon approximately 2 tablespoons of the butter on ovenproof plate & place in oven until the butter is completely melted.

Remove the plate from oven & place a large piece of warm pie right over the melted butter.

Top the pie with a scoop of vanilla ice cream then, top with the hot fudge & caramel toppings. Sprinkle with chopped or crushed walnuts; serve immediately & enjoy.

Nutrition: Calories: 178 Fat: 76 g Carbs: 67.8 g Protein: 76.9 g Sodium:929 mg

Skillet Chocolate Chip Cookie

Preparation Time: 30 minutes

Cooking Time: 20 minutes

Servings: 8 to 10

Ingredients:

1 pouch chocolate chip cookie mix (17.5-ounce)

Hot fudge, for drizzling (store-bought or homemade)

⅓ cup chocolate chips, semi-sweet, for sprinkling

1 stick (½ cup) softened butter, unsalted

Ice cream for serving

1 large egg

Directions:

Lightly coat a 10" ovenproof skillet with the cooking spray; set aside and then Preheat oven to 350 F.

Add the cookie mix together with butter & egg to a medium-sized bowl; give the ingredients a good stir until a soft dough form.

Evenly spread the dough in skillet, smoothing with a rubber spatula.

Evenly sprinkle with the chocolate chips, pressing them down lightly using your fingertips.

Bake until the edges turn light golden brown, for 20 to 23 minutes. Ensure that you don't over bake

Place the skillet over a cooling rack & let cool for 5 minutes then drizzle with the hot fudge; serve with the ice cream.

Nutrition: Calories: 233 Fat: 87.8 g Carbs: 57.6 Protein: 65. 7 Sodium: 867 mg

Timeless Restaurant Favorites

Starbucks® Mocha Frappuccino

Preparation Time: 10 minutes

Cooking Time: 10 minutes

Servings: 8

Ingredients

¾ cup chocolate syrup

4 cups milk

¾ cup sugar

3 cups espresso coffee

For Topping:

Chocolate syrup

Whipped cream

Directions

Prepare the coffee as per the directions provided by the manufacturer.

Mix hot coffee & sugar in a mixer until the sugar is completely dissolved, for a minute or two, on high settings.

Add chocolate syrup & milk; continue to mix for a minute more.

For easy storage, pour the mixture into a sealable container. Store in a refrigerator until ready to use.

Now, combine mix & ice (in equal proportion) in a blender & blend until smooth, on high settings & prepare the drink.

Pour the drink into separate glasses & top each glass first with the whipped cream & then drizzle chocolate syrup on the top.

Serve & enjoy!

Nutrition: Calories: 197 kcal Protein: 4.54 g Fat: 4.47 g

Carbohydrates: 35 g

Reese's Peanut Butter Cups

Preparation time: 15 minutes

Cooking time: 2 minutes

Chill time: 6 hours

Servings: 10

Ingredients

Salt, pinch

1½ cups peanut butter

1 cup confectioners' sugar

20 ounces milk chocolate chips

Directions

Take a medium bowl and mix the salt, peanut butter, and sugar until firm.

Place the chocolate chips in a microwave-safe bowl and microwave for 2 minutes to melt.

Grease the muffin tin with oil spray and spoon some of the melted chocolate into each muffin cup.

Take a spoon and draw the chocolate up to the edges of the muffin cups until all sides are coated.

Cool in the refrigerator for few hours.

Once chocolate is solid, spread about 1 teaspoon of peanut butter onto each cup.

Leave space to fill the edges of the cups.

Create the final layer by pouring melted chocolate on top of each muffin cup.

Let sit at room temperature until cool.

Refrigerate for a few hours until firm.

Remove the cups from the muffin tray and serve.

Nutrition: Calories 455 Total fat 21.7 g Carbs 59 g Protein 9.7 g Sodium 384 mg

Cadbury Cream Egg

Preparation time: 15 minutes

Cooking time: 2 minutes + Chill time: 3 hours 30 minutes

Servings: 6

Ingredients

⅓ cup light corn syrup

⅓ cup butter

2 teaspoons vanilla

⅓ teaspoon salt

3½ cups white sugar, ground and sifted

3 drops yellow food coloring

2 drops red food coloring

16 ounces chocolate chips, milk

3 teaspoons vegetable shortening

Directions

Take a bowl and combine corn syrup, butter, vanilla, salt and powdered sugar.

Mix all the ingredients well with a beater.

Reserve ⅓ of the mixture in a separate bowl, then add food coloring.

Chill both portions in the refrigerator for 2 hours.

Form rolls from the orange filling, about ¾-inch in diameter.

Wrap the orange rolls with white filling.

Repeat until all of the mixture is consumed.

Form in the shape of eggs.

Let sit in the refrigerator for 1 hour.

Melt the chocolate chips in the microwave.

Dip each egg roll in the melted chocolate.

Cool in the refrigerator for 30 minutes.

Once solid, serve and enjoy.

Nutrition: Calories 1004 Total fat 34.8 g Carbs 174 g Protein 5.9 g Sodium 261 mg

Loaded Potato Skins from TGI Friday's

Preparation Time: 30 minutes

Cooking Time: 7 minutes

Servings: 6

Ingredients

1 teaspoon oil

6 medium-sized potatoes

1 cup vegetable oil

8 ounces Cheddar cheese, grated

3 strips thick cut cooked bacon, diced

16 ounces sour cream

1 ripe tomato, diced

Fresh chives for serving, chopped finely

Directions:

Preheat oven to 375°F. Line a large baking sheet with parchment paper.

Using a fork, prick potatoes in a few places. Microwave for at least 10 minutes or until soft.

Halve the potatoes vertically and remove the insides of the potato until there is only ¼ inch of the potato shell left.

In a deep saucepan, heat oil to 365 °F. Deep-fry potato shells for 5 minutes, then transfer onto plate lined with paper towels.

Add cheese and diced bacon into potato shells. Place on the baking sheet prepared earlier and bake for at least 7 minutes or until cheese is fully melted.

Serve immediately with spoonful of sour cream on top or on the side. Sprinkle with diced tomatoes and chives.

Nutrition: Calories 519 Total Fat 33 g Carbs 41 g Protein 17 g Sodium 361 mg

Avocado Eggrolls from The Cheesecake Factory

Preparation Time: 15 minutes

Cooking Time: 5 minutes

Servings: 8

Ingredients

Cilantro dipping sauce:

¾ cup fresh cilantro leaves, chopped

⅓ cup sour cream

2 tablespoons mayonnaise

1 garlic clove

2 tablespoons lime juice

Salt and pepper, to taste

Egg roll:

1 cup vegetable oil

3 avocados, peeled and seeded

1 Roma tomato, minced

¼ cup red onion, minced

2 tablespoons fresh cilantro leaves, diced

2 tablespoons lime juice

Salt and pepper, to taste

8 egg roll wrappers

Directions:

Mix together the ingredients for the cilantro dipping sauce in a bowl. Set aside.

Preheat a large pot with oil over medium-high heat. Oil temperature should reach 350°F and there should be enough oil to cover the rolls, about 3 to 4 inches deep

Mash avocados in a bowl. Mix in tomato, red onion, cilantro, and lime juice. Add salt and pepper, to taste.

Position avocado mixture onto the middle of an egg roll wrapper. Fold wrapper on top of mixture and roll until the mixture is fully wrapped. Secure edges of the wrapper by pressing with water using your finger. Repeat for the remaining mixture and wrappers.

Deep-fry rolls in the pot of hot oil for at least 2 minutes or until all sides are golden brown.

Remove from pot with tongs and place onto a plate lined with paper towels.

Serve with the cilantro dipping sauce on the side.

Nutrition: Calories 288 Total Fat 18 g Carbs 28 g Protein 6 g Sodium 219 mg

Copycat Bloomin' Onion and Chili Sauce from Outback

Preparation Time: 20 minutes

Cooking Time: 4 minutes

Servings: 8

Ingredients

2 large sweet onions such as a Vidalia

Oil for frying

Seasoned flour:

1 cup flour

2 teaspoons paprika

1 teaspoons garlic powder

¼ teaspoon pepper

⅛ teaspoon cayenne

Chili sauce (yields 2 ¼ cups):

1 cup mayonnaise

1 cup sour cream

¼ cup tomato chili sauce

¼ teaspoon cayenne

Dipping Sauce:

½ cup mayonnaise

2 teaspoons ketchup

2 teaspoons horseradish cream

¼ teaspoon paprika

¼ teaspoon salt

⅛ teaspoon dried oregano

1 dash black pepper

1 dash cayenne

Batter:

⅓ cup cornstarch

1½ cups flour

2 teaspoons garlic, minced

2 teaspoons paprika

1 teaspoon salt

1 teaspoon pepper

24 ounces beer

Directions:

Preheat a large pot with oil over medium-high heat until 375 °F, not exceeding 400 °F.

In a large bowl, mix together the ingredients for the seasoned flour.

In a separate bowl, mix together the ingredients for the chili sauce.

For the dipping sauce, mix the ingredients together in a bowl and keep refrigerated.

To make the batter, combine cornstarch, flour, garlic, paprika, salt, and pepper in a bowl. Mix well.

Pour in beer to the bowl of dry ingredients. Blend well until smooth.

Chop off ¾ inches of the onion on the top. Peel, then slice until just above the bottom root end to make about 14 vertical wedges. Take out about 1 inch of petals from the inside.

Coat petals in flour, then shake off any excess. Dip in batter. Make sure the onion is well-coated.

Deep-fry for about 1 to 3 minutes, or until golden brown.

Transfer onto plate lined with paper towels to drain.

Serve with chili sauce and dipping sauce on the side.

Nutrition: Calories 404 Total Fat 12 g Carbs 59 g Protein 8 g Sodium 436 mg

Deep Fried Pickles from Texas Roadhouse

Preparation Time: 10 minutes

Cooking Time: 10 minutes

Servings: 4

Ingredients

Vegetable oil, for deep frying

¼ cup flour

1¼ teaspoons Cajun seasoning, divided

¼ teaspoon oregano

¼ teaspoon basil

⅛ teaspoon cayenne pepper

Kosher salt

2 cups dill pickles, drained and sliced

¼ cup mayonnaise

1 tablespoon horseradish

1 tablespoon ketchup

Directions:

Preheat about 1½ inches oil to 375°F in a large pot.

In a separate bowl, make the coating by combining flour, 1 teaspoon Cajun seasoning, oregano, basil, cayenne pepper, and Kosher salt.

Dredge pickle slices in flour mixture. Lightly shake to remove any excess, then carefully lower into hot oil. Work in batches so as to not overcrowd the pot. Deep fry for about 2 minutes or until lightly brown.

Using a slotted spoon, transfer pickles to a plate lined with paper towels to drain.

While pickles drain and cool, add mayonnaise, horseradish, ketchup, and remaining Cajun seasoning in a bowl. Mix well.

Serve immediately with dip on the side.

Nutrition: Calories 296 Total fat 28 g Saturated fat 14 g Carbs 12 g Sugar 4 g Fibers 0 g Protein 1 g Sodium 1201 mg

The Famous Breadsticks from Olive Garden

Preparation Time: 15 minutes

Cooking Time: 15 minutes

Servings: 16

Ingredients

1½ cups plus 2 tablespoons warm water

1 package active dry yeast

4¼ cups all-purpose flour, plus more for dusting

2 tablespoons unsalted butter, softened

2 tablespoons sugar

1 tablespoon fine salt

3 tablespoons unsalted butter, melted

½ teaspoon kosher salt

¼ teaspoon garlic powder

Pinch dried oregano

Directions:

Preheat oven to 400°F. Prepare a baking tray and line it with parchment paper.

To prepare the dough, pour ¼ cup warm water in a mixing bowl. Add yeast and wait 5 minutes or until bubbles form. Combine with flour, 2 tablespoons butter, sugar, salt, and 1¼ cups and 2 tablespoons warm water. Mix for about 5 minutes or until mixture turns into dough that is a bit sticky.

Remove from bowl and transfer onto a flat surface sprinkled with flour. Knead for about 3 minutes until dough is soft and smooth. Form dough into a log that is about 2 feet long. Then, cut dough equally in 1½-inch long pieces, making 16 small pieces in total. For each piece, knead slightly and form into a breadstick that is about 7 inches long. Position breadsticks on prepared baking tray with 2-inch spaces in between each. Cover, then set aside for 45 minutes or until dough size has doubled.

Using a brush, coat breadsticks with 1½ tablespoons melted butter. Season with ¼ teaspoon salt.

Place in oven and bake for 15 minutes or until slightly golden.

As the breadsticks bake, mix remaining salt, garlic powder, and oregano in a bowl.

Remove breadsticks from oven and immediately coat with the rest of the melted butter. Season with herb mixture.

Serve warm.

Nutrition: Calories 146 Total fat 4 g Saturated fat 2 g Carbs 25 g Sugar 2 g Fibers 1 g Protein 4 g Sodium 456 mg

Hot n' Spicy Buffalo Wings from Hooters

Preparation Time: 15 minutes

Cooking Time: 12 minutes

Servings: 2

Ingredients

½ cup flour

¼ teaspoon paprika

¼ teaspoon cayenne pepper

¼ teaspoon salt

10 chicken wings

Vegetable oil, for deep frying

¼ cup butter

¼ cup Louisiana hot sauce

1 dash ground black pepper

1 dash garlic powder

Blue cheese salad dressing

Celery cut into sticks

Directions:

In a bowl, add flour, paprika, cayenne pepper, and salt. Mix well.

In a separate bowl, add chicken wings. Lightly coat with flour mixture. Make sure the coating for each wing is even. Refrigerate for at least 1 hour to keep the coating attached while frying.

To prepare, preheat about 1½-inch deep oil in deep fryer to 375°F.

In a separate small pot, heat butter, hot sauce, pepper, and garlic powder. Stir until butter is dissolved and ingredients are well mixed.

Carefully lower coated chicken wings into the hot oil. Deep fry for about 10 to 15 minutes or until wings turn partly dark brown then transfer onto a plate lined with paper towels to drain.

While the wings are still hot, transfer to a bowl and pour hot sauce mixture on top. Toss to coat all wings evenly.

Serve hot with blue cheese dressing and celery sticks.

Nutrition: Calories 867 Total fat 63 g Saturated fat 26 g Carbs 25 g Sugar 1 g Fibers 1 g Protein 49 g Sodium 1419 mg

Southwestern Eggrolls from Chili's

Preparation Time: 10 minutes

Cooking Time: 20 minutes

Servings: 4

Ingredients

1 chicken breast, boneless and skinless

8 cups plus 2 tablespoons vegetable oil, divided

2 tablespoons red bell pepper, finely chopped

2 tablespoons scallion, finely chopped

⅓ cup frozen corn

¼ cup canned black beans, rinsed and drained

2 tablespoons frozen spinach, thawed and drained

2 tablespoons pickled jalapeno peppers, chopped

½ tablespoon fresh parsley, finely chopped

½ teaspoon ground cumin

½ teaspoon chili powder

¼ plus ⅛ teaspoon salt, and more to taste

Pinch cayenne pepper

¾ cup jack cheese, grated

5 6-inch flour tortillas

1 egg, beaten

¼ cup avocado, mashed

¼ cup mayonnaise

¼ cup sour cream

1 tablespoon buttermilk

1½ teaspoons white vinegar

⅛ teaspoon dried parsley

⅛ teaspoon onion powder

Pinch dried dill weed

Pinch garlic powder

Pinch pepper, plus more to taste

2 tablespoons tomato, diced

1 tablespoon onion, diced

Directions:

Preheat grill to high heat.

Coat chicken breast with 1 tablespoon vegetable oil and season with salt and pepper. Grill for about 4 to 5 minutes on each side or until cooked through. Set aside and wait until cool. Then, chop into small cubes. Set aside.

Heat 1 tablespoon vegetable oil in a pan over medium-high heat. Stir fry red pepper and scallions for a few minutes, just enough for the vegetables to become soft. Add cooked chicken, corn, black beans, spinach, jalapeño peppers, parsley, cumin, chili powder, salt, and cayenne pepper. Cook for an additional 4 minutes. Stir until all the ingredients are mixed well.

Remove from heat and stir in cheese until melted.

Microwave tortillas wrapped in a damp cheese cloth for about 10-20 seconds on high.

For each of the five rolls, add about ⅕ chicken and vegetable mixture onto the middle part of a tortilla. Fold the edges inwards and roll tightly over the mixture. Before closing the wrap, brush egg onto the inner edge to help seal the tortilla...

Position rolls on a plate with the sealed edges facing down. Wrap everything in plastic wrap and place in the freezer. Freeze for at least 4 hours or overnight.

To prepare, preheat 8 cups oil in deep fryer to 350°F.

Prepare dipping sauce by mixing avocado, mayonnaise, sour cream, buttermilk, white vinegar, remaining salt, dried parsley, onion powder, dill weed, garlic powder, and pepper in a bowl. Set aside.

Carefully lower egg rolls in deep fryer. Cook for about 8 to 10 minutes then transfer to a plate lined with paper towels. Allow to cool for 2 minutes or until cool enough to handle.

Slice each roll diagonally lengthwise. Serve with dipping sauce garnished with tomato and onion.

Nutrition: Calories 655 Total fat 45 g Saturated fat 22 g Carbs 40 g Sugar 2 g Fibers 6 g Protein 26 g Sodium 655 mg

Conclusion

For meals that are scheduled to be eaten at least three days after cooking, freezing is a great option. Freezing food is safe and convenient, but it doesn't work for every type of meal. You can also freeze the ingredients for a slow cooker meal and then dump out the container into the slow cooker and leave it there. This saves a lot of time and means you can pre-prep meals up to 1-2 months in advance.

The last food safety consideration you need to make with regards to meal prepping is how you reheat food. Most people opt to microwave their meals for warming, but you can use any other conventional heating source in your kitchen as well. The reason people love the microwave for heating their meal prep meals is that it's quick and convenient.

However, you have to be careful with microwaving because over-cooking can cause food to taste bad. To combat this, cook your food in one-minute intervals and check on it between each minute. You can also help your food cook more evenly and quickly but keeping your meat cut into small pieces when you cook it. You should never put food directly from the freezer into the microwave. Let your frozen food thaw first when it's possible.

Food reheating and prep safety will become second nature over time. Meal prep can be overwhelming and require a lot of thought and patience, but it becomes a lot easier once you get used to it. Many of the mistakes are easy to avoid.

However, mistakes do happen, and as such, it's best to cook for short periods rather than longer ones, so you have less of a risk of making a mistake and needing to scrap everything you have prepared for that substantial amount of time. While it is a lot and seems complicated, meal prepping is the best way to set yourself up for success using your delicious copycat recipes. Make the meals using double the products and adjust the times; that is all it is to it!

Don't store hot food in the fridge. Keep your refrigerator at the proper temperature (should be below 40º Fahrenheit). If your refrigerator is warmer than this, it promotes the growth of bacteria. Any drastic temperature changes will cause condensation to form on the food items. You need to let your prepared food cool down in the open air - before putting it in a container and closing the lid. The increased moisture levels can open the door to bacteria growth.

Label the Containers: There are some other things you have to consider when freezing your meals. You should always label your container with the date that you put it in the freezer. You also need to double-check that your bottles, jars, or bags are each sealed tightly. If your containers aren't air-tight, your food will become freezer burnt and need to be trashed.

These recipes are the perfect additions to your daily meals. If you want affordable restaurant-style food, then here is the answer. We've got recipes from all your favorite restaurants. If you ever host a party, there are dishes in here that will make your guests ask, "Hey, what's the recipe for that chicken your served?" If you regularly cook for yourself or your family, then these simple recipes will help you elevate your meals. And if you just love having restaurant food at home, then try making some yourself—you never know, you might even be a better cook!

By cooking at home, you get to save money and time, you get to control portions, and you get to customize each meal. Remember, the recipes found here are more of a guide ultimately, you get to choose how your next meal will taste and how best to prepare it.

If you're looking for healthier substitutions for some ingredients, here is a conversion chart that you can refer to:

Healthier Substitutions and Conversions

White bread	Whole-wheat bread
Butter, margarine, shortening or oil to prevent sticking	Cooking spray or nonstick pans
Cream cheese	Fat-free or low-fat cream cheese, fat-free ricotta cheese
Cheese	Low-fat or fat-free cheese
Eggs	Two egg whites or ¼ cup egg substitute for each whole egg
White flour	Whole-wheat flour for half of the called-for all-purpose flour
Ground beef	Extra-lean or lean ground beef, chicken or turkey breast
Whole milk	Evaporated skim milk, reduced-fat or fat-free milk
Pasta	Whole-wheat pasta
White rice	Brown rice, wild rice, bulgur, or pearl barley
Salad dressing	Fat-free or reduced-calorie dressing or flavored vinegars
Salt	Herbs, spices, fruit juices or salt-free seasoning mixes or herb blends

Syrup	Pureed fruit, such as applesauce, or low-calorie, sugar-free syrup

Standard U.S./Metric Measurement Conversions

VOLUME CONVERSIONS	
U.S. Volume Measure	Metric Equivalent
1/8 teaspoon	0.5 milliliters
¼ teaspoon	1 milliliters
½ teaspoon	2 milliliters
1 teaspoon	5 milliliters
½ tablespoon	7 milliliters
1 tablespoon (3 teaspoons)	15 milliliters
2 tablespoons (1 fluid ounce)	30 milliliters
¼ cup (4 tablespoons)	60 milliliters
1/3 cup	90 milliliters
½ cup (4 fluid ounces)	125 milliliters
2/3 cup	160 milliliters
¾ cup (6 fluid ounces)	180 milliliters

1 cup (16 tablespoons)	250 milliliters
1 pint (2 cups)	500 milliliters
1 quart (4 cups)	1 liter (about)

WEIGHT CONVERSIONS	
U.S. Weight Measure	Metric Equivalent
½ ounce	15 grams
1 ounce	30 grams
2 ounces	60 grams
3 ounces	85 grams
¼ pound (4 ounces)	115 grams
½ pound (8 ounces)	225 grams

¾ pound (12 ounces)	340 grams
1 pound (16 ounces)	454 grams

OVEN TEMPERATURE CONVERSIONS	
Degrees Fahrenheit	Degrees Celsius
200 degrees F	100 degrees C
250 degrees F	120 degrees C
275 degrees F	140 degrees C
300 degrees F	150 degrees C
325 degrees F	160 degrees C
350 degrees F	180 degrees C
375 degrees F	190 degrees C
400 degrees F	200 degrees C
425 degrees F	220 degrees C
450 degrees F	230 degrees C

Hopefully, these recipes have given you a few tips and tricks on how to recreate your favorite restaurant dishes at home. The book is meant to give you some motivation and inspiration to cook these meals in the comforts of your own home.

CPSIA information can be obtained
at www.ICGtesting.com
Printed in the USA
BVHW041525131120
593255BV00016B/868